A HISTORY
of
JAPANESE THEOLOGY

A HISTORY
of
JAPANESE THEOLOGY

Edited and
translated by

Yasuo Furuya

WILLIAM B. EERDMANS PUBLISHING COMPANY
GRAND RAPIDS, MICHIGAN / CAMBRIDGE, U.K.

© 1997 Wm. B. Eerdmans Publishing Co.

255 Jefferson Ave. S.E., Grand Rapids, Michigan 49503 /

P.O. Box 163, Cambridge CB3 9PU U.K.

Printed in the United States of America

01 00 99 98 97   7 6 5 4 3 2 1

Library of Congress Cataloging-in-Publication Data

A history of Japanese theology / edited and translated by Yasuo Furuya.

p.   cm.

Includes bibliographical references.

ISBN 0-8028-4108-2 (pbk.: alk. paper)

1. Theology, Doctrinal — Japan — History.   I. Furuya, Yasuo, 1926-

BT30.J3H57   1997

230′.0952 — dc20   96-43366

CIP

Contents

Introduction

THIS IS THE FIRST BOOK on the history of Japanese theology ever to be written by Japanese themselves. It was the American professor of theology Carl Michelson who introduced Japanese theology to the world outside Japan for the first time in his *Japanese Contribution to Christian Theology* (1960). Michelson begins his preface with the following remarks:

> Protestant Christianity is only one hundred years old in Japan. That means the Japanese church is one of the younger churches in Christendom. Yet, of all the younger churches, it is apparently the first to have developed a significant theology. For the last twenty-five years there has been emerging among these people a theological climate that is expressing itself today in several commanding points of view. (p. 9)

Since more than thirty-five years have elapsed since the above was written, readers might expect that by now there must be a book on the history of Japanese theology written by Japanese themselves. But no single book has yet appeared.

In 1966 the first book on the history of Japanese theology was published by Charles H. Germany, a former American missionary to Japan, with the title *Protestant Theologies in Modern Japan*. As its subtitle indicates, it is "a history of dominant theological currents 1920-1960." The book was so well done that it was translated into

1

Japanese; however, it has some limitations. It covers only Protestant theology, neglecting Roman Catholic theology. Furthermore, the author's main interest is in "the nature of the influence that various theologies had upon the church's understanding of her responsibility to society" (p. xii).

Why, then, has no history of Japanese theology ever been written by the Japanese, while there are several books on the history of the Japanese church and Japanese Christianity by others? To be sure, there is a book entitled *History of Japanese Christian Theological Thoughts* (1968), by Yoshitaka Kumano (1889-1981). Note, however, that it does not say "theology," but "theological thoughts." Why? According to Kumano, who has written three volumes of dogmatics, the Japanese church has not yet sufficiently grown up to have a "history of Japanese theology." In order to have *theology* in the traditional Western sense of the word, the Japanese church must have doctrines, ethics, rituals, etc., upon which theology can be established. The Japanese church, however, has existed so far without the need of doctrines and church orders in the strict sense. This theological immaturity is not necessarily due to any defects of faith or of the church in Japan. Rather, Kumano thinks it is due to the following three reasons that he finds in the historical background of the Japanese church.

The first reason is that since the Japanese church tried from the beginning to be a self-supporting church, independent of foreign missions, it has no strong denominational theological foundations. The second reason is that since the Japanese church has close relations with American churches, the sense of historical and theological ties with the Reformation is rather weak. The third reason is that, as a consequence, the Japanese church has no strong theological traditions. Only the Apostles' Creed and the common doctrines of Protestant churches, such as justification by faith, are regarded as traditions. For these three reasons, concludes Kumano, the Japanese church has produced theological thoughts, but not yet a theology in the strict sense of the word (*Complete Works of Yoshitaka Kumano,* vol. 12, p. 6).

Now, the question is: What is theology in the strict sense of the word? Unless a church becomes like the European church, or to use Ernst Troeltsch's typological term *Kirche,* or state church, is a church incapable of producing theology? Ken Ishihara, (1882-1976), who was regarded as the dean of academic studies of Christianity in Japan for many years, would say "no" without any hesitation to this question. This elder historian of Christianity pointed out the following four characteristics of Japanese Christianity.

The first is that Japanese churches have had a negative attitude towards denominationalism from the beginning. They are skeptical about denominational differences in doctrine and orders. In this sense, all Japanese churches belong more or less to the "Non-church" (Mukyokai) type. The second characteristic is that there is a lack of a legal understanding of the church. This may be due to the general characteristic of the Japanese people, who are not law conscious. Japanese Christians, consequently, are not enthusiastic about the laws and regulations of the church. A third characteristic is the Japanese church's evangelical and biblical attitude, derived from the first missionaries, who were influenced by Methodism in England, Revivalism in America, and Pietism in eighteenth-century Germany. As a result, the Japanese church became active in social and moral movements, embracing asceticism. The fourth characteristic is the lack of a clear concept of the church. Although the general teaching, thoughts, lifestyles, and customs of Christianity have been accepted, Christianity as the church has not yet been well established (*Collected Works of Ken Ishihara*, vol. 10, pp. 211-218).

To sum up, Ishihara says that there is not yet a clear understanding of the concept of the church in Japan. He notices that a similar situation also exists in America; however, it is not so dangerous there since America is already a Christian society, although Americans do not have much respect for tradition, and do not readily trust authority. However, Japan is a pagan society. If the concept of the church is not clear and unambiguous, this is difficult and dangerous for the church's very existence. Accordingly, Ishihara insists on using the concept of the church in the strict, traditional sense of the word; otherwise, the idea of the church will be confused and its real meaning lost.

There is a close connection, according to Ishihara, between the absence of a clear concept of the church and the lack of a clear understanding of the Christian faith among Japanese Christians. The theological dilemma of Japanese Christians is not that they are unable to understand, for example, the theological thinking of Barth and Bonhoeffer, but that there is as yet an absence of the sensitivity and human maturity needed to understand and empathize with their convincing cry, based upon their experiences. In other words, says Ishihara, "Christian understanding is shallow and Church life impoverished, owing to an immature superficiality. This is why there are so many 'half Christians', who sometimes behave like Christians, but who usually live in an old life-style" (*Collected Works,* p. 217).

This idea of Ishihara's reminds us of the German philosopher Karl Löwith (1897-1973), who came to Japan in 1936 to teach for five years at Ishihara's invitation. On the basis of his teaching experience and observation of his colleagues in Japan, he made critical comments such as the following:

> Die Art und Weise, wie der Japaner das europäische Denken zumeist übernimmt, scheint uns fragwürdig, sofern wir sie nicht als echte Aneignung ansehen können. . . . Die Studenten studieren zwar mit Hingabe unsere europäischen Bücher und sie verstehen sie auch dank ihrer Intelligenz, aber sie ziehen aus ihrem Studium keine Konsequenzen für eigenes, japanisches Selbst. Sie unterscheiden nicht und vergleichen nicht die europäishchen Begriffe, z.B. 'Wille', 'Freiheit', und 'Geist', mit dem, was ihnen in ihrem eigenen Leben, Denken und Sprechen entspricht, bzw. von diesen abweicht. Sie lernen das an sich Fremde nicht für sich selbst. Sie leben wie in zwei Stockwerken: einem unteren, fundamentalen, in dem sie japanisch fühlen und denken, und einem oberen, in dem die europäischen Wissenschaften von Platon bis zu Heidegger aufgereiht stehen, und der europäische Lehrer fragt sich: wo ist die Treppe, auf der sie von einem zum andern gehen? (*Sämtliche Schriften,* vol. 2, pp. 536f.)

> [The way in which the Japanese, for the most part, accept European thought seems doubtful to us, insofar as we cannot regard it as genuine assimilation. The students certainly study our European books with dedication, and thanks to their intelligence, they understand them; but they fail to draw any consequences from them for their own Japanese identity. They do not make distinctions or comparisons between European terms, such as *will, freedom,* and *spirit,* and corresponding concepts in their own life, thought and speech, or where they differ from them. They do not learn what is strange to them for its own sake. They live on two stories, as it were: a lower, fundamental one, in which they feel and think in the Japanese

manner, and an upper one, in which they line up with European knowledge from Plato to Heidegger, and the European teacher wonders: Where is the staircase, to take them from the one to the other?]

Ishihara was, of course, not unaware of this kind of criticism. He wrote in his essay, "The Task of Japanese Theology" (1959), as follows:

> We are quite aware, and even feel ashamed that Christianity in Japan is, like other cultures, sciences and arts, an imitation of that of Western countries. . . . It is true that many preachers speak about the Gospel, imitating the sermons and theology of Western countries. Is this, however, entirely blameworthy? I am afraid that they would make more mistakes if they used Japanese parables and analogies. I think that imitation is inevitable, and that it is safer, although we do have to be careful about how we imitate. (pp. 203f.)

Both Kumano and Ishihara, therefore, were very cautious in talking about the history of Japanese theology, although neither of them was satisfied with imitation; and they looked forward to seeing the establishment of theology, in the strict sense of the word, in Japan.

A further reason why there has so far been no book on the history of Japanese theology written by a Japanese theologian is suspicion of "Japanese theology" and caution in talking about it. At the beginning of his essay "The Task of Japanese Theology," Ishihara wrote:

> First of all, I read the title as "the task of theology *in* Japan." For me, the concept of Japanese theology does not exist, and I cannot accept it. What kind of task faces theology *in Japan?* I cannot consider the theme of this essay, except in terms of this question. (p. 193)

This negative view of "Japanese theology" is quite common among Japanese theologians because this term reminds them of the theology of "Japanese Christians," rather like the "Deutsche Christen" who had cooperated with militarism during World War II. These people tried to Japanize theology by mixing Christianity with Shintoism. This is why Japanese theologians are reluctant to use terms such as "Japanese theology," or even "Asian theology."

5

However, a postwar generation has emerged that is rather critical of the older generation's view of theology in the strict German sense of the word, meaning only dogmatics, e.g., Karl Barth. It was Hideo Ohki, then a young lecturer in theology, who first demanded the liberation of Japanese theology from "Germanic Captivity." In 1961, shortly after his return from America, where he had studied under Reinhold Niebuhr, he wrote a short essay about his professor, whom he called paradoxically "a great theologian who is not a theologian." Ohki concluded this essay with these words:

> If one were to learn from Niebuhr, one would liberate the theology of Japan from futile "Germanic captivity." One's own theology will become independent, and will have the ability to face up to the realities of Japanese history rigorously. In particular, one will break the dead-lock of Barthianism in Japan (which has existed from the pre-war through to the post-war periods), and will restore theology to a realism which is in close touch with the reality of the Church. (*Kobun,* Nov. 1961, p. 5)

The echo of Ohki's plea for the liberation of Japanese theology from Germanic captivity was heard not only by other young American-educated theologians, but also by young German-educated theologians, such as Seiichi Yagi. More favorably disposed towards Japanese theology than Ohki, Yagi wrote in anger as follows:

> At one time the infant Japanese theology needed Western theology as its guardian. . . . Our long dependence has fostered bad habits. Some people have even declared that they would not read any theological works written by Japanese. . . . There is a regrettable tendency among us of being ashamed of referring to Japanese studies in the bibliographies appended to our books. . . . We can never hope for a healthy growth of Japanese theology under such circumstances. . . . It is therefore with good reason that the cry has recently arisen among young theologians: "Deliver Japanese theology from Germanic captivity." (*Japan Christian Quarterly,* Fall 1964, p. 259)

More than thirty years have passed since these young theologians demanded liberation from "Germanic Captivity." They are no longer young, but are now senior scholars who have produced many theological works, which they themselves consider to be their own creations rather than imitations. This book will go some way toward answering the question of whether we have now come of age and are able to write a history of Japanese theology.

Toward another question, whether "Japanese theology" exists or not, this book maintains an open mind. We do not wish to judge the question ourselves. We do not believe in the myth of the so-called uniqueness of Japanese culture, and we insist on demythologizing it. It is not we ourselves but people outside Japan who can judge whether or not there is a uniquely Japanese theology. So "Japanese theology" in the title of this book means the same as "theology in Japan."

Readers will find that most of the theologians dealt with in this book are Protestants. It is not our intention to write only about Protestant theology, but about an ecumenical one, including Roman Catholic and Greek Orthodox theologies. But why are Protestants so dominant in Japanese theology? According to the statistics reported in The *Christian Yearbook, 1988,* Christians number about one million, a little less than one percent of the population. Of these, 627,000 are Protestants, 428,000 are Catholics, and 25,000 are Orthodox. There is, therefore, not a great difference in the numbers of Protestants and Catholics. The main reason that the majority of theologians are Protestants lies in the past history of the Japanese churches.

The first missionaries who came to Japan in 1549 were Catholics. They built the oldest theological schools, *seminario,* in 1580 — one in Arima in Kyushu, and another in Azuchi near Kyoto. But after the success of the so-called Christian Century in Japan, Christianity was banned, and theological education, whose foundations had just been laid, came to a complete stop. It was not until 1862, two hundred years after the expulsion of the missionaries, that Catholic missionaries came back to Japan. They reopened theological schools in 1870; however, unlike the newly arrived Protestant missionaries from America, French Catholic missionaries could not attract young people, especially students and intellectuals. This is why it took such a long time before Japanese Catholics took the leadership in the church hierarchy and in theology. Before the Second World War there were very few Japanese Catholic theologians. It was not until after the 1960s that Japanese Catholic theologians began to emerge alongside Catholic popular novelists. Even today, there are very few recognized theologians among the Orthodox.

Protestant Christianity came to Japan for the first time in 1859 with the American missionaries. The oldest Protestant theological school was Doshisha. Founded in 1875 by Congregationalists, it still exists as the Theological School of Doshisha University in Kyoto. The next one was the Union Theological Seminary, which was established in Tokyo in 1877 with a Presbyterian, Reformed background. This tradition was merged into the present Tokyo Union Theological Seminary, which was founded by the United Church of Christ (Kyodan) during the war by the union of many denominational theological schools. After the war, as several denominations left the Kyodan, each denomination established its own theological schools. Some Christian universities also established theological schools, although two of them were closed down during the 1970s after the university disturbances.

Needless to say, theological schools and seminaries are not the only places where theology is in the making. Who the people engaging in theology are, and where they are active, may be learned by looking at the Japan Society of Christian Studies, the largest and most inclusive academic organization of theologians. Founded in 1952, it publishes an annual journal, *Theological Studies in Japan*. As of 1988, the total membership of the society was 597, including 546 men and 51 women. Eighty-three percent are Protestants, and 10 percent are Catholics. Seven percent are teaching in theological seminaries or schools, while 47 percent are teaching at Christian universities and colleges. Nine percent are teaching in government universities, while another 9 percent are at private, secular universities and colleges. Many of those who are teaching in non-Christian schools do not teach theology, but other subjects, such as languages and the history of philosophy. Eleven percent of the members of the society are church pastors. Of course, there are many clergy who are interested in theology, but who are not members. The numbers of clergy in Japan are as follows: Protestant, 10,800; Catholic, 10,500; Orthodox, 80.

We begin the history of Japanese theology, therefore, at the time when the first Protestant missionaries came to Japan in the nineteenth century. The whole history, though short, may be divided into four periods, according to four theological generations. The first period (chapter 1) is the first generation of Christians, born in the 1850s and early 1860s, who began the study of theology. The second period (chapter 2) is the second generation, born in the 1880s and 1890s, who were students of the first generation. The third period (chapter 3) is the period after World War II, in which the third generation began to engage in theological works. The fourth period is the most recent (chapter 4), in which the fourth generation joins with the third generation.[1]

In order to understand the historical background of these periods, we recommend the reading of the following works:

1. Drummond, Richard H.: *A History of Christianity in Japan* (Grand Rapids: Wm. B. Eerdmans, 1971), which deals with Protestants, Catholics, and Orthodox alike.
2. Iglehart, Charles W.: *A Century of Protestant Christianity in Japan* (Tokyo: Charles E. Tuttle, 1959).
3. Phillips, James M.: *From the Rising of the Sun: Christians and Society in Contemporary Japan* (Maryknoll, NY: Orbis Books, 1981), which discusses the conflicts and divisions within the Japanese churches around 1970.

For the sake of consistency, in this book we follow the practice adopted in these books of always giving surnames, whether Japanese or Western, last.

---

1. Incidentally, there exists a Japanese calendar, based upon the Imperial period. Although some Christians are opposed to the use of this calendar, it is common practice to speak of the Meiji period (1868-1912), the Taisho period (1912-1926), and the Showa period (1926-1989).

CHAPTER 1

The First Generation:
Christian Leaders in the First Period

AKIO DOHI

THE FIRST GENERATION of Christian leaders were born in the middle of the nineteenth century into the feudal society of Japan. They became Christians during a period of turmoil, which began with the Meiji Restoration in 1868. The four who are especially deserving of attention are Danjo Ebina (1856-1937), Masahisa Uemura (1858-1925), Hiromichi Kozaki (1856-1938), and Kanzo Uchimura (1861-1930). Since these four represent such a wide variety in their personalities and thinking, looking at them more closely will enable us to draw a general picture of theological trends among the first generation of Christians.

The Acceptance of Christianity
by Japanese in the Earliest Period

The overseas missions of Anglo-American Protestant Christianity in the eighteenth and nineteenth centuries represented a new development. Overseas missions grew out of revival movements that challenged Enlightenment ways of thinking and that reacted against the stagnation from which Christianity was suffering as a result of becoming an established religion. At the same time, mission was a religious and cultural activity, borne out of the process of establishing political, economic, and military domination by the Western powers over the non-Western

11

world. The Anglo-American missions took India, Southeast Asia, and China as their first fields of activity, and only later Japan and Korea.

From the seventeenth century onwards, fearing the combination of Roman Catholic missions and the territorial expansionist policies of Western countries, Japan had shut off the nation and continued to ban Christianity. In 1858, however, Japan was forced by America to open up the country and to sign a treaty of amity with Western countries. In the following years, missionaries from America and Great Britain arrived from Anglican, Reformed, Presbyterian, Baptist, and Congregational churches. By the time of the Meiji Restoration, feudalism had been broken down, and Japan became a modern state. Since the government paid no attention to the Christian missions, in 1873 missionaries from the Methodist churches in North America and from the Allgemeiner Evangelisch-Protestantischer Missionsverein also arrived.

Members of Japanese society in general, however, were never friendly towards Christianity. Previously they had expelled it, because they thought that Christianity would destroy Japan's traditional religion, morality, and social customs. Although this time Japan imported modern Western civilization in order to enrich and strengthen herself, the majority of those intellectuals who accepted utilitarianism and evolutionism were indifferent or even hostile to Christianity.

Some of them, however, did accept Christianity. These were people who had belonged to the warrior class in the feudal society. They had received a Confucian education and took the ethical view that they should not be misled by their own interests and desires, but instead should respect some cause and commit themselves to serving their feudal lord. They were conscious of their own elite status, discussing the destiny of the nation and the government of the people. However, they belonged to the feudal clans who had been defeated in civil war. Because of the modernization of Japanese society, they had lost their social status as warriors. In order to overcome their difficulties and to achieve future fame in the world, they wanted to acquire Western knowledge.

At that time, the only foreigners who could teach Western science and culture were Christian teachers. Among them were a number of missionaries. Since they were not allowed to preach the gospel directly, they served as school teachers. While imbibing Western knowledge from these teachers, some Japanese students became interested in the Christianity underlying their teachers' personalities, and they became Christians themselves. Through the examples of the four people already mentioned above, we will look at how they became Christians and examine their understanding of Christianity, because they were highly influential in directing the path that theology was to take in Japan.

Danjo Ebina (1866-1937)

Danjo Ebina was born in Northern Kyushu. As the son of a warrior, he was educated to serve the feudal lord and even to die for him without fear. However, as a result of the Meiji Restoration, the feudal clan was abolished, the lord's castle was burned down, and a young prince died. Ebina underwent a kind of spiritual death, and he began to seek a new lord to serve.

In 1872 Ebina entered the Kumamoto Western School in central Kyushu. This school had been opened by a group of "enlightened" people. An American, Leroy Lansing Janes, a committed Christian, was invited to teach there. While reading the books of enlightened Confucianism, Ebina came to the conclusion that the "heaven" of Confucianism was not a rational but rather a personal one, like the God of Christianity. From Janes he learned natural science and history. While attending a Bible study led by Janes, he came to feel the working of a God who created and ruled everything. When he learned from Janes that prayer, in the form of communication with God and addressing requests to him, was an obligation all creatures owed their Creator, he was shocked. Having lost a lord to serve, he had been living a self-centered life. Now he realized that he was to serve God, the Creator of all. For him, God was his lord, and he was his subject; he understood the relationship between lord and subject as a moral one.

About thirty students from this school, including Ebina, accepted Christianity, as taught by Janes. In 1876 they all climbed a small hill together at Kumamoto and took an oath that they would proclaim Christianity and so enlighten people and explain the fairness and justice within Christianity in order to be loyal to the nation. As the result of the sensation caused by the students' action both inside and outside the school, it was closed down. Before this, Janes had commended Ebina and the other students to the Doshisha School. This Christian school had been founded by Jyo Neesima in 1875 with the cooperation of missionaries from the American Board of Commissioners for Foreign Missions.

While studying at Doshisha, Ebina underwent a new religious experience. He tried to deny all his desires in order to serve God alone; however, he could not deny his intellectual desires for the sake of evangelizing Japan. This raised a problem for him. Finally, he came to discover his deep desire to seek God the Father as his child. With this self-awareness, he fought against sin and became convinced that man can overcome all his desires if he becomes united with God. To describe this relationship with God, he used the expression *Fushi Ushin* (ethics of the father-son relationship), one of the five basic moral precepts taught by Confucianism. This way of understanding his religious experiences shows that Ebina thought of Christianity as analogous to Confucianism.

In this way Ebina tried to prove that Christianity was a universal truth, valid for the Japanese way of life in a Confucian world. In later years, he also thought of Christianity in relation to Shintoism in the same way. Shintoism's respect for God is similar to Christianity's piety. He insisted that if Shintoism were purified, it would become Christianity. In this attitude, however, and in the way it ignored the differences between Confucianism, Shintoism, and Christianity, there was a danger that the unique character of Christianity might be denied. Throughout his life, Ebina constructed his theology around his personal religious experience, and this danger became increasingly obvious. We will discuss this point further below.

Hiromichi Kozaki (1856-1928)

Hiromichi Kozaki was also born the son of a warrior of the Kumamoto clan and underwent a Confucian education. He entered the Kumamoto Western School one year before Ebina. At school he already showed his powers of leadership and ability to manage a business. He also became a Christian at this time. However, as he later explained, this did not mean giving up Confucianism, since he regarded Christianity as the fulfillment of the spirit of Confucianism. Analysis of what he meant by this shows that his thinking was radically different from Ebina's.

Having followed Confucius's teaching to "keep the gods at a respectful distance," Kozaki tried not to come too close to Shintoism and Buddhism. He was proud of his Confucianism, and was convinced that he had no need to learn about Christianity from Janes, although he did study Western knowledge. However, when he saw students becoming Christians under Janes's influence in spite of persecution, he felt that Christianity had supernatural powers. When he saw Janes praying in tears for Japan, he was impressed and decided to learn about Christianity. With his Confucian background, he could understand the idea of the existence of God and the immortality of the soul. He could not, however, believe in the Bible's stories of miracles, in Christ's divinity, or in salvation through the cross. This caused him difficulties. One day, in answer to Kozaki's questions, Janes quoted 1 Corinthians 2:11 and told him that the question of God was beyond human, rational cognition, and that unless he received God's spirit, he could not understand God. Janes then recommended that he pray directly to God. This led to his believing the Christian gospel.

Unlike Ebina, Kozaki did not seek to find common religious ground between Confucianism and Christianity. Having been inspired by Janes, he could break through Confucian reason; through God's spirit, he could accept the Christian revelation. Thus, in accepting the Trinitarian God and salvation through Christ, he went further than Ebina. Reading Henry W. Beecher and Horace Bushnell deepened his understanding of Christianity.

How did Kozaki see the relationship between Confucianism and Christianity? In his book *A New Essay on Politics and Religion* (1886), he contrasts these religions. For example, though Confucianism speaks of evil and of the necessity of finding a way out of it, it does not teach salvation, as does Christianity. Confucianism is limited to one nation, and speaks of the distinction between upper and lower classes and high and low ranks. In Christianity, the kingdom of God is extended to all nations, and the gospel preaches the equality of all people. Confucianism, however, is not unrelated to Christianity, nor does it contradict it. Like Judaism, Confucianism prepares the way for Christianity. Awareness of one's own sin in Confucianism can be connected with salvation in Christianity. When Confucianism's teaching about loyalty and filial piety is applied to the God of Christianity, the meaning of belief in God and obedience to him becomes clear. Thus Christianity goes beyond

15

Confucianism; it perfects and fulfills it. These ideas of Kozaki's remove the possibility of the dangers implicit in Ebina's approach. However, since Kozaki accepted Christianity through Confucianism, traces of Confucianism remained in his ideas and actions. He thought that Christianity could provide a spiritual principle for a modern nation, just as Confucianism had been effective in forming the order of a feudal society. He gave Christianity a place in the doctrines of an emperor-led nation which sought to enrich and strengthen itself and which engaged in the invasion and conquest of other Asian nations.

Masahisa Uemura (1861-1925)

Masahisa Uemura was born the son of a direct feudal vassal of the Tokugawa Shogunate. As a result of the Meiji Restoration, his father lost his social status, and his family fell into financial difficulties. Thereafter, Uemura was encouraged by his mother, who said: "Since you are the son of a warrior, be a strong man, found a house, and rise to fame." He was deeply impressed by her exhortation. In the development of his ideas, the value system of a warrior, with its pride, will-power, the honor of the family name, and filial piety, played an important role. Full of youthful ambition, he went to Yokohama, where he could study Western knowledge. He entered a private school run by James H. Ballagh, a missionary from the Dutch Reformed Church in America. It was here that he also accepted Christianity. Recollecting the time of his conversion, he wrote:

> I entered the school when the meetings of the Week of Prayer were taking place, and I was introduced to Christ's teachings. The first sermon I ever listened to was on the Pentecostal outpouring of the Holy Spirit. The missionary's Japanese was difficult to understand, but somehow the Christian idea of God, which seemed to me so odd and new, took possession of my soul. The idea was grand and elevating. A new world was opened to the worshipper of the hero-god, Kato Kiyomasa. My youthful soul was stormed by the wonderful faith in the one true God, always and everywhere present, holy and merciful. Without any discussion, and before making any enquiries, I felt myself to be already a Christian. . . . It was not until

some time after my first conversion that the sense of sin and of forgiveness, through the atonement of Christ, came to be properly appreciated. *(Retrospect by a Convert of 1872)*

Needless to say, this religious experience did not lead him to accept everything in Christianity. Although he could understand the Christian view of God quite well, he could not easily appreciate the meaning of sin and its forgiveness through atonement. In 1873 he was baptized in a Yokohama church and entered a theological school directed by Samuel R. Brown, a missionary from the same denomination as Ballagh. Through the life of the church and his studies at the theological school, he gradually overcame his "grave doubt." Having been born into poverty, both economically and spiritually, he had experienced the bitter hardness of the world. He also realized that within himself there were all kinds of sin and evil, such as craftiness, jealousy, greed, and deception. He could, however, experience the solution of the problem of these sins through Christ's atonement. His early book, *A Guide-Post to the Gospel* (1885), was a plain explanation of sin and the way of salvation.

The interesting point here is the way that Uemura came to an understanding of the gospel: through listening to sermons in church and studying theology at a theological school. This process was different from that of Ebina, to whom we have already been introduced, and Uchimura, who will be described below. These two learned Christianity from their teachers, who were Christians, and came to understanding through suffering and inward struggles. Deepening their understanding of Christianity in this way, they then went on to preach it to others. Although Uemura also underwent spiritual suffering, he found a solution within the church and carried out his theological activities within the tradition of the church. This difference will become clearer when we examine below a theological controversy that arose between Ebina and Uemura.

What happened to Uemura's youthful ambition? He abandoned the idea of raising his family's reputation through worldly success. Instead, he wanted to become a Christian evangelist, and he hoped to found churches all over the country as a church leader. He also wanted to become a prophet of justice and humanity in society. He understood "Bushido" (the way of the warrior) as a way of commitment to the great cause of social justice, insisting on its purification by Christianity. He also changed the traditional idea of filial piety into Christian filial piety directed towards God the Father, and interpreted the Christian way of life as the practice of this filial piety towards God. Thus, Uemura renewed traditional values through Christianity and clarified the way and direction of faith and life for Japanese Christians.

Kanzo Uchimura (1861-1930)

We can learn about Kanzo Uchimura's early life from several translations of his own book, *How I Became a Christian* (1895). He, too, was born the son of a warrior in Edo (Tokyo), and grew up conscious of his warrior status and of Confucian morality. He followed the ways of Japanese folk religion, worshiping gods and observing taboos. After learning Western science in several schools in Tokyo, in 1877 he entered Sapporo Agricultural School, which had been founded by the government to train leaders for the development of Hokkaido, Japan's northern island. The headmaster of this school had been William S. Clark, whose strong Christian belief and insight shone through his teaching. Clark drew up a statement that students were asked to sign called "Covenant of Believers in Christ," which proclaimed belief in the grace of God and demanded a strict ethical life. Uchimura did not learn directly from Clark, who had already left for America; nevertheless, he was almost forced to sign this covenant by senior students. However, this led to his finding himself anew. Until then, he had been afraid to observe and analyze nature, believing in nature as the world of the gods and subject to their curse. Now, through belief in God, he was freed from the bondage of the gods, and was able to observe nature as nature and to see the mystery of God's creation within it. He then turned his attention to the theory of evolution and saw his life's work as explaining the relation between Christian theism and the doctrine of evolution.

Another problem to which Uchimura turned his attention was the position of Japanese Christians. Those Japanese who had survived the end of feudalism and had lived through the early years of the development of modern Japan were very nationalistic. They maintained that Christianity was not compatible with traditional Japanese values. Uchimura was a contemporary of these people, and he was also a great patriot. At the same time, however, he was a Christian. He tried to live in two "J's", i.e., Jesus and Japan. He believed that the love of Jesus purified love of Japan, and that love of Japan clarified the love of Jesus and also gave people a goal in life.

What Uchimura learned from Clark and others was the noble and strict ethical life of Christians. For him, Christian ethics was the realization of the ethics of the warrior, and the Christian life represented the practice of Confucian morality. He tried to live a life of Christian purity by his own efforts. However, the more he tried to live purely, the more he was aware of impurity within himself, and this distressed him. After leaving school, Uchimura became a civil servant. Troubled by the conflict between Christian and official ethics, he eventually resigned from government service. A further problem was the failure of his marriage.

In 1884 Uchimura went to America and worked in a hospital, modeling himself on Martin Luther, who subjected himself to discipline in the monastery in Erfurt. On Jyo Neesima's recommendation, he went to study at Amherst College. There he came to know the college president, Julius Seelye, a man of noble and gentle personality, imbued with deep insight. Through him, Uchimura came to an evangelical faith. Seelye taught him that he should not just think about himself and worry about his struggle with evil and sin, but should look up to Jesus Christ, who was crucified for our sins, and then live trusting fully in God. Uchimura was filled with joy at believing in the gospel. After further studies at Hartford Theological Seminary, he returned to Japan.

These four men became Christian evangelists, the first three as ministers, and the last one as founder of the Non-church. They all had to face the difficulties of undertaking evangelism in Japan as Japanese Christians, a task for which theological work was indispensable.

The Disturbance Caused by the New Theology

At the beginning of the 1890s, a theological storm was blowing up within the Japanese church. Although its immediate cause was the arrival of missionaries who brought with them the new theological tendencies current in Europe and America, its deeper cause was already to be found within the church in Japan.

As we have already noted, the Protestant churches in Japan were founded in the 1870s as the result of the efforts of the denominational missions of English and American churches. At this time, Japan was being transformed into a modern state. It was therefore necessary for the Japanese church to become independent, with its own denominational doctrine, organization, and missionary policy. There were, however, two possible ways for this development to take place.

The first was to accept the traditions of the denominations that lay behind the missions. Even if those churches that had similar denominational backgrounds were to unite, they could still remain loyal to the denominational tradition of the past. This was the case with the Holy Catholic Church in Japan (Anglican, established in 1887), The Japan Methodist Church (established in 1907), and the Lutheran and Baptist Churches. To their members, the obvious policy was to form a denominational church, and their task was to deepen their understanding of their denominational tradition. As long as they continued in this direction, there was little risk of any theological conflict developing.

The second policy was to develop a denomination that would be, to some extent, unique to Japan, even if it had been founded by the mission branch of an overseas denominational church. The Japanese Presbyterian Church and the Japanese Congregational Church belong to this category. These churches had a stormy passage, because in their attempts to create a uniquely Japanese denomination and tradition they had to negotiate with the missions and come to terms with their denominational traditions. A handicap was their comparative immaturity.

Another factor leading to the storm was the influence of the Great Awakening, introduced into Japan by American Christians, which succeeded in penetrating and breaking down denominational barriers. The founding spirit of the American Board was itself a product of the Awakening. Furthermore, because of the strong anti-Christian feeling at that time, unity among Christians was vital, since they were a minority in Japanese society. Some local Japanese churches or congregations founded after 1872 had nothing to do with any foreign denominations. They insisted on a simple creed, with a common name and organization. However, since their nondenominationalism and identity were vague, they had little more to offer than a form of idealism, and they did not survive. The atmosphere produced by this movement persisted for many years in the form of communication among Christians, for example, and in cooperation between churches.

The course followed by the Japanese Presbyterian Church was a very difficult one. At the beginning, their intention was to found a non-denominational church. In 1877, as soon as they realized that this was impossible, they joined several other churches in forming the Union Church of Christ in Japan, at the initiative of missionaries from the Reformed and Presbyterian missions. Having been under Reformed and Presbyterian influence for many years, in 1890 they founded Nihon Kirisuto Kyokai (The Church of Christ in Japan), reaffirming a non-denominational origin unique to Japan. Unlike the first type of denominations, they had many difficulties to face in their formation. At the outset, many churches related to the American Board and to Dishisha tried to be nondenominational community churches. However, since denominational mission churches had been founded in many areas, they formed Nihon Kumiai Kyokai (The Associated Churches in Japan) in 1886. Although they regarded their church as a denomination unique to Japan, they followed the congregational model, advocating the freedom and self-government of each local church with mutual cooperation between them. The creed written into the constitution at the time of the church's formation, however, was not congregational in character, but consisted of the Doctrinal Basis adopted by the meeting that led to the foundation of the Evangelical Alliance in London in 1846. Since that creed was already in use by the churches, there was no objection to including it in the constitution. However, the significance it had for each church and for each individual was not clear. Members and adherents of this church were, accordingly, in a condition where the impact of the New Theology might easily be felt.

What was known as "New Theology" was a liberal and rational tendency within theology introduced from Europe and America in the late 1880s. In 1885, Wilfred Spinner, a missionary from the Evangelisch-Protestantischer Missionsverein, arrived in Japan. This missionary society had been founded the previous year by church leaders in Germany and Switzerland who were members of the Religionsgeschichtlichte Schule. Their aim was to spread Christianity and its culture to non-Christian peoples by making contact with those elements of the truth that they already possessed. In 1887 Arthur M. Knapp from the American Unitarian Association arrived, followed by George L. Perin from the Universalist

General Convention in 1890. These groups denied the traditional doctrine of the Trinity and Christology. Though the churches developed by these missions in Japan remained small, their theological impact upon Japanese Christian leaders was great. They accepted the Bible as the word of God in a naive evangelical way, and regarded other religions from an exclusive point of view.

Hiromichi Kozaki was the first to respond to this New Theology, but we will return to him later. Michitomo Kanamori (1857-1945) was wholly won over by it. After graduating from Doshisha, he engaged in evangelical work in Tokyo. He published a book, *Liberal Theology* (1892), which was a free translation of *Religionsphilosophie auf geschichtlicher Grundlage* by Otto Pfleiderer, a supporter of the Allgemeiner Evangelisch-Protestantischer Missionsverein. His own book, *The Present and Future of Christianity in Japan* (1891), was an exposition of the New Theology. Its main points are as follows: Although there are various religions in Japan, a religion of truth and life will triumph. However, one religion or denomination cannot monopolize the truth of religion. So far as Christianity is concerned, the Bible's miracle stories, the prohibition of smoking and drinking, the imported denominational disputes from foreign countries, and the ritualization of Christianity are stumbling blocks for Japanese people. Its claims of the Bible as the only true revelation, the divinity of Christ, and atonement through the cross may contain some elements of truth. However, its external forms are wrapped up in primitive religious concepts, which should be discarded. Modern knowledge demands this.

How, then, should the Bible be understood? It is not the infallible verbal revelation of God, but a collection of Jewish religious writings. It is a primary source for nurturing religious feelings in human beings. It teaches a harmonious union with God, which is a religious truth. Though this truth is not only to be found in the Bible, the Bible shows it most clearly. The claim that the divinity of Christ is confirmed by miracles, by prophecies, by his sinlessness, and by the influence he has had cannot be proved historically. Jesus was an extraordinary religious man, given special gifts by God, who lived in harmonious union with God. Nevertheless, one cannot make him God. Such a belief, according to the New Theology, is derived from the primitive religious ideas of ancient peoples. The idea of atonement through Christ, it was believed, arose in the same way. The penal-substitution theory is nothing but an application of the human relationships found in ancient societies. Although orthodox faith insists that we should believe these doctrines, they are unacceptable. The salvation offered by Christianity lies in harmonious union between God and human beings, and Christ is a forerunner of this salvation.

In 1892 Kanamori told the General Assembly of the Associated Churches that he would resign from the church because his views were incompatible with those of the majority of the church. The Assembly accepted his resignation. At the same time, it approved the Confession of Faith drafted by Kozaki, which consisted of brief articles of faith, such as the trinitarian God, the dual nature of Jesus Christ, the Atonement, and the authority of the Bible. Whether the Confession had any binding power was not discussed, so its status remained ambiguous. Some people who disagreed with the Confession remained in the church, while others left. Kanamori himself left the church and became active in the business world and in government. However, in 1915 he returned and undertook mass evangelism both inside and outside Japan.

It was Masahisa Uemura of the Church of Christ in Japan who saw through the problems of the New Theology. Seeing that it might shake the foundations of the faith of his denomination, he confronted it vigorously. He tackled the problem in the monthly journal *Japan Critics* and in a weekly newspaper, *Evangelical Weekly* (which changed its title to *Evangelical News* in 1891), both of which had been founded in 1890. Uemura rejected the verbal infallibility of the Bible and accepted academic works in biblical criticism and comparative religion of German theology. However, he could not agree with Kanamori's views. In his article "Contemporary Christianity and Future Christianity" (*Japan Critics*, 1891, 7), he criticized Kanamori for being too hasty in counterattacking the doctrines of the Bible and the divinity of Christ. Christianity, he asserted, is an "absolute religion" and unchangeable, based upon a historical fact, i.e., Jesus Christ. Christianity educates and nurtures Japanese people with noble and pure ethics. There is no need to adopt, as Kanamori insisted, anything from other religions. Though Kanamori criticized the miracles related in the Bible, wrote Uemura, Christianity without miracles is like Christianity without Christ, as the resurrection of Christ clearly shows. Turning to the issue of the slavish imitation of foreign countries, Uemura argued that the Japanese church and its theology showed an independent spirit, and they were working hard to eliminate imitation — it was just a matter of time. While Kanamori claimed that the Bible deals with the religion of the Jewish people, Uemura maintained that the Bible is the life of Christianity throughout history. Christian theology is a science that makes God's revelation clear, based upon the facts of history contained in the Bible. Biblical criticism makes the historical nature of revelation clear. While Kanamori said that the study of comparative religion shows that Christianity stands on the same level as other religions, the truth, wrote Uemura, is that it shows that differences exist, and that when other religions reach the level of Christianity, then they become perfect. Kanamori abandoned evangelical Christianity, Uemura declared, and instead adopted a vague, ethical theism incapable of nurturing noble religious feelings or of guaranteeing the love of God.

Since Kanamori's reaction to Uemura's criticism was not made public, no open theological dispute resulted. Most likely, Uemura could not understand why Kanamori rejected the evangelical nature of the church in his acceptance of the New Theology. Confident of the basis upon which the Japanese church stood, he was quite sure that the future would be bright if the present direction and trends could be developed and deepened. From Uemura's point of view, Kanamori appeared to be a man who had adopted strange ideas imported from foreign theology. Whether the two controversial issues of (1) the absolute claims of Christianity, raised by the Religionsgeschichtliche Schule, and (2) the relations between evangelical faith and the results of biblical criticism could be dealt with as Uemura thought is an open question.

The Theological Controversy between Ebina and Uemura

From the outset, Japanese Christians practiced fellowship and cooperation among themselves. From 1878 onward the National Christian Laymen's Fellowship Meeting was held every few years. It was reorganized in 1885 as the Japan Christian Alliance. Later, when it joined the World Evangelical Alliance, it became the Japan Evangelical Alliance. Responding to the Twentieth Century Forward Movement of the Anglo-American churches, the Alliance planned and carried out mass evangelism in the years 1901-1902. This large-scale systematic evangelism was activated by a revival that grew out of meetings held in Tokyo. However, because of differences in belief revealed among preachers at these meetings, many in the audiences were perplexed.

Masahisa Uemura raised a question. He said that the Evangelical Alliance was an organization for fellowship, not for evangelism. It was no wonder that different ideas were put forward by the preachers at these meetings. If the Alliance really wanted to carry out evangelism, he said, it should have cleared up the question of the basic understanding of the faith. Uemura mentioned Ebina by name in his article, thus questioning his position. This led to a controversy between the two men which lasted for five months between 1901 and 1902.

Unlike the discussions that took place between Kanamori and Uemura, this controversy was concerned directly with doctrinal issues, such as the relation between God and Christ and the Incarnation. It had considerable significance for the basic faith of the church. At this time the churches were gradually becoming more definite denominational organizations whose members consisted mainly of the urban middle classes, which were increasing in numbers with the growth of capitalism. As evangelical programs were being planned by individual denominations as well as on a cooperative basis, this controversy was timely for determining what should be proclaimed to other people. We will not describe the progress of the controversy here, merely the views of each disputant, beginning with Ebina.

Ebina had no intention of denying the divinity of Christ or the Trinity. "I believe," he said, "in the divinity of Christ and the divinity of the Holy Spirit, and I also believe that the doctrine of the Trinity contains profound religious truth." However, he was opposed to Uemura's way of thinking, which clung to the historically transmitted creeds, and tried to solve problems on the strength of these beliefs. He was convinced that "the essence of Christianity is not a doctrinal creed, but the life of Christ" (*The Essence of Christianity,* 1903). Jesus and the apostles did not preach doctrines like the Trinity, which are used to judge whether people are believers or not. The doctrine of the Trinity and the Incarnation of the Logos are nothing but explanations of the religious consciousness of Christians in the ancient world. Nobody can turn their assertions into eternal and unchangeable truth.

As already mentioned, Ebina understood the relationship between God and man in terms of the Confucian ethics of the relationship between father and child, which was a fundamental part of his religious understanding. On the basis of this understanding, he argued as follows:

> The reason why Christ was aware that his relation with God was an ethical father-child relation, was that there was an ontological father-child relationship in his person. The reason why there was an ethical father-child substance in Christ, was that there was in his person something equal to the ousia of God. There is no doubt about this. . . . I cannot help but recognize the substance of the heavenly Father in Christ. This seems to me to be so, because he is God's child, who indeed has the substance of God. Christ has two aspects. He is man towards God, and God towards man. To have these two aspects, is to have the substance of the real God-man.

From this one sentence alone, Ebina's view seems to be close to the Nicene Creed, which regarded Christ as being of one substance *(homoousios)* with God the Father, and to the Definition of Chalcedon, which insisted on both the divine and human natures of Jesus Christ. However, this is not the case. He does not agree with Uemura, who regards Christ as God, saying, "Christ is God-man." If God became man, then this God is no longer God. Accordingly, Christ is not God. If Christ is the Son who is at the same time God, then this leads to tritheism, consisting of God the Father, God the Son, and God the Holy Spirit. Ebina could not, therefore, accept the doctrine of the Trinity, nor of the *persona* of Christ, who is at the same time God and man.

Why was this his attitude? The reason, as already stated, was that his analysis was based upon his personal religious experience. Out of his spiritual agony, feeling that he was weighed down with sin in God's eyes, he came to an awareness that he was part of a father-son relationship with God. He thought that everybody shared this awareness. He regarded Jesus Christ as a person with strong religious feelings who ultimately came to this religious awareness, and who lived in union with God. "If one regards the person of Christ as representing ultimate goodness for mankind, then it is evident that he is also God." What is important to note in this is that Ebina regarded Jesus Christ as "the ultimate goodness for mankind." In this sense, Jesus is merely a man. As he said later, "the difference between Christ and us is not one of substance, but in the degree of development." Because Jesus ultimately realized the father-child relationship with God, he became Christ and God. Thus we see that Ebina's view is close to adoptionism, in which Jesus is a mere man, but becomes a son of God through God's power (dynamism). He was, therefore, unable to accept Uemura's view that "God became man and came down to earth."

In this respect Ebina's ideas are not in accordance with the traditional teaching of Christianity that Jesus is the once-for-all and unique revelation of God. This seems to be because Ebina's theology was heavily dependent upon Confucian ways of thinking. In Confucianism, logic, which identifies Shanti (God) with nature, is correlated with human ethics. This kind of naturalism is strong in Ebina's thought. He regards the father-child relationship as a universal that exists as religious awareness linking God, Jesus Christ, and man. Consequently, God's revelation in history through Christ loses its uniqueness and is rationalized as a pattern open to humanity in general. Jesus Christ is not God, but represents the highest form of the religious man. However, he did increase human awareness of God's way, which is universal, and he did achieve union with God. These are the problems that arise when one tries to construct Christian theology in an Asian or Japanese way of thinking.

Uemura had a high regard for Ebina as a person, but criticized his views vigorously. His counter-argument was as follows. For Ebina, Christianity was the highest form of awareness of the father-child relationship, based upon his own experience. It follows that the relation between Christ and Ebina becomes like that between an older and younger person, and Christ is no longer a savior who redeems the sins of humanity. Ebina says that God shows his love in Christ, and man comes to know the love of God in Christ. This love is seen in the redemptive action of Christ, who offered himself as a sacrifice on the cross. This act of Jesus is God's act. Therefore, unless one recognizes Christ as God, one cannot know the love of God. However, Ebina maintains that every man has something divine within him, and so Christ shares this divinity, too. Although he says that he sees the love of God in Christ, his view of God and man is based upon an ambiguous pantheistic argument. Uemura went on to say:

> Mr. Ebina does not believe in the deity of Christ. His Christianity does not regard Christ as God, and does not worship him. We believe

that Christ is God. Christ is God who became man. We believe in the immanence and omni-presence of Christ. We worship Christ and offer him prayer. Mr. Ebina looks up to Christ only as a teacher. We do that, but we also believe that he is the Saviour.

Uemura had good reason to believe in the atonement of Christ. He had earlier written a book entitled *The Outline of Truth* (1884) in which he argued that man has a religious sense which leads him to seek God, who rules and orders everything, and to live in a relationship with him. Because of this religious sense, humans have the will to elevate their character towards God. However, the more one tries to achieve this, the more one learns of sin through one's own experience. Sin has an irresistible power which causes humans to lose sight of their purpose and which separates them from God. This is why they need to receive forgiveness of sins through the cross of Christ, through God's grace toward humankind. By doing this, humanity can live in relationship with God and can fulfill his will.

Uemura's own convictions were expressed in these words: "We believe that God became man, He came to this world, died on the Cross, and redeemed man's sin. And we believe that Jesus Christ is the only Son of the living God, who receives the prayers and worship of mankind." This faith is the historical faith of the church, upheld by Christians for centuries. Ebina's views are not in accordance with this faith. According to Uemura, if one fully understands Jesus' words as recorded in the Gospels and the witness of the apostles, then the first Christians believed that Christ was God and they worshiped him as such. Early Christianity's doctrines of the Logos and the Incarnation arose naturally out of this faith. They were not the results of speculative study on the part of early Christians.

Having criticized Ebina's views in this way, Uemura wrote a series of fourteen articles with the collective title "Christ and His Works" in his weekly journal, *Evangelical News,* in order to present his own views positively. "Christianity is Christ. What is most important in Christ is his divinity and incarnation." In saying this, he was insisting on the importance of clarifying the person and work of Christ. He then tried to prove that the apostles praised and worshiped Christ as God, taking his evidence from the New Testament, especially the Pauline and Johannine Epistles, and the Epistle to the Hebrews. According to Uemura, the basis of their faith was the divinity of Jesus, his sinlessness, and the supernatural nature of his resurrection. He is very cautious in the way he uses the lives of Jesus by liberal theologians such as David F. Strauss, Alois E. Biedermann, and Adolf von Harnack. However, according to Yoshitaka Kumano, Uemura's arguments do not deserve to be considered as academic studies, but as "apologetics of an edifying character." Considering the situation of the Japanese church at that time, Kumano's appraisal would appear to be fair and reasonable.

For instance, Uemura says that Paul made Christ "inferior to God." Referring to Paul's First Epistle to the Corinthians, in which he writes, "the head of a woman is her husband and the head of Christ is God," Uemura goes on to say:

> Though man and woman are of the same kind, there is a distinction between them, and their ways are not the same. Among mankind, who are equal by nature, there is a relation of subordination. This is true of the relationship of Christ to God. Though Christ is really divine, and he is one with the Father, he cannot but be subordinate to the Father, because he is the Son. The Son respects, serves and follows God the Father, showing filial piety.

In these words, Uemura tries to make it clear that Christ is to be served as Lord, but at the same time has to serve as a servant. There is no difficulty in this. However, when he explains the relationship between God and Christ in terms of the relationship between man and woman, as expounded in Paul's theology and also as analogous to the filial piety of Confucianism, this may seem similar to the "subordination" found in Origenism, which was rejected by the Council of Nicaea (325 AD). Uemura says that the Christology of the apostles is summarized in the Nicene Creed. In 1904 he founded the Tokyo Theological School, and remained its president until his death. In his lectures on systematic theology, which were printed as a series in *Evangelical News* (8 May 1926–4 August 1927), he also uses words such as "the way of filial piety" and "subordination."

As we have seen, the ideas of Ebina and Uemura were in sharp contrast. Speaking of Ebina's view of the Trinity, Uemura said that Ebina could not understand Christ's salvation because he did not clearly grasp the problem of sin. In reply to this, Ebina spoke out of his own religious experience, saying that the basis of sin is self-centeredness. Christ's salvation means turning aside from self-centeredness to God-centeredness, through the cross of Christ. The origin of the differences between them lies in the methodology of their respective theologies. Ebina understood his religious experience in terms of Confucian logic and interpreted the Bible and various doctrines subjectively on the basis of this understanding. Uemura, on the other hand, subordinated his experience to evangelical tradition and developed his ideas objectively on the basis of the Bible. Because of these differences, their ideas could not be brought into line with each other. Each insisted on maintaining his own opinions and attacked those of the other.

A decision of the Conference of the Evangelical Alliance held in 1902 in connection with this controversy had unfortunate results. This conference defined evangelicalism as belief in Jesus Christ, who as God was made incarnate for human salvation. This meant that Uemura's ideas were approved. However, confusion arose between the role of the Evangelical Alliance and a creedal church. The conference's decision was reached in violation of its own rules, and by underhanded political maneuvering. Confusion and turmoil was the result, and the men who were elected president and vice-president of the Alliance refused to accept office. When the Evangelical Alliance was dissolved into the Federation of Churches in 1912, no definition of evangelicalism was written into the new constitution.

The Theology of Hiromichi Kozaki

As we have seen above, Hiromichi Kozaki accepted Christianity as the religion of revelation, which went beyond Confucian reason. Since he regarded Confucianism as a preparation for Christianity, and Christianity as the perfection and fulfillment of Confucianism, his understanding of Christianity was strongly characterized by Confucianism. His view of the relationship between the theory of evolution and Christianity was also affected by this outlook.

The theory of evolution had a great impact upon political theory and on Christianity in the early years of modern Japan. Kozaki learned of the problems associated with this theory first at Doshisha from John T. Gulick, an American Board missionary, and secondly from Henry Faulds, a Scottish Presbyterian missionary, when Kozaki was undertaking evangelistic work in Tokyo. He concluded that there was no contradiction between the theory and the Bible, but that the theistic theory of evolution was in harmony with the Bible.

Kozaki continued to pay attention to this issue. In his article "The Theory of Evolution and Christianity" (1903), he argued that the question was no longer how to harmonize evolutionism and theism, but how to accommodate the logic of evolution to Christianity. He also saw the logic of evolution as a parable of heaven, as growth from the seed to the fruit. In the modern world, this logic was allied to human development and the progress of history into a total worldview. As a result of this, our worldview changed, he argued, from a static to a dynamic one. In the past the universe was regarded as dead, being ordered by God through natural law. Now, however, the universe has come to be regarded as a living thing in which God is immanent, and which is still being developed by God. Therefore, through God's immanence and guidance, human activities such as politics, economics, and culture come to have religious significance. Kozaki suggested that the logic of evolution could be applied to the doctrine of the Holy Spirit as well. The church was founded through the descent of the Holy Spirit and developed by its grace. The Holy Spirit is immanent in the church, and directs it. In this way, our experience of faith is deepened, and the life of faith is stimulated.

It is thus clear that Kozaki's evolutionary way of thinking determines his understanding of Christian doctrine, and, on the other hand, mankind's rational perceptions are limited by his faith as a Christian in the work of God and the Holy Spirit. For Kozaki, faith and reason are not in conflict with each other, but are mutually interdependent. He calls the outcome of this relationship "reason sanctified by the Holy Spirit."

What kind of theology did this "reason sanctified by the Holy Spirit" lead to, taken as his standpoint of faith? Kozaki always criticized the theory of the infallibility of the Bible. In 1889 the first Summer School was held at Doshisha with students, young people, and church leaders coming from all over Japan. Kozaki gave a lecture there called "The Inspiration of the Bible." Referring to the views of George T. Ladd of Yale University and Joseph H. Thayer of Harvard, he went on to develop his own ideas. According to him, to say that the Bible was inspired by God does not mean that its words are literally infallible. Biblical inspiration means that it was written under the guidance of the Holy Spirit.

"The 'inspiration' of the Bible is the influence of the spirit of God. God's spirit does not work on things, but on human beings, not on words but on the heart, not on the external but on the internal." Accordingly, we should not concern ourselves with the personalities of the writers of the Bible or their methods of writing. Instead we must understand the importance of the facts recorded in the Bible, namely, "The Son of God became incarnate and lived among us, and was finally crucified for mankind. This is the great joy which concerns all human beings."

As Kozaki later said, it was at about this time that he began to think about his "reason sanctified by the Holy Spirit." The Summer School lecture made it clear that he formulated this idea while developing his views on the Bible. However, this lecture did not fully explain what he meant by this expression.

Kozaki took a great interest in the controversy between Ebina and Uemura. In 1902 he wrote an article, "A Reading of Ebina's View of the Trinity," for the *Tokyo Weekly News,* of which he was the editor. In this article he argued that the issue of Christology was a matter of life and death for the church, and he criticized Ebina's views as not being in accordance with the essence of Christianity. He went on to say that such views would prevent the healthy growth of the Japanese church. He also questioned Ebina's allegation that his own view was derived from his religious awareness of Jesus, whereas the church fathers in the period after the second century emphasized the doctrine of the Trinity. This doctrine was derived from the Hellenistic concept of the logos, which had nothing to do with the religious awareness of Jesus, according to Ebina. In opposition to this, Kozaki argued that through the immanence of the Holy Spirit and its guidance of the church, the germs of Christology, and the doctrine of the Trinity as developed by the early church were already to be seen in the Gospels and Epistles. Gradually they were accepted as dogma. In this sense, said Kozaki, these dogmas are the products of "reason sanctified by the Holy Spirit." In developing these dogmas, the church fathers interpreted the apostolic tradition referring to Jesus in the spirit of Hellenism. Kozaki thus sought to find the true relationship between faith and reason in his own way.

In 1911 he published a book, *Das Wesen des Christentums* (The essence of Christianity). This is his most characteristic work, and provides a summary of his ideas to date. The book was also meant to defend evangelicalism against the New Theology. Those issues which divided

Japanese Christians, such as the relationship between Christianity and science, the relationship between Christianity and other religions, the infallibility of the Bible, Christology, and the Atonement, arose because it was not yet clear what the essence of Christianity really was. His own view is very clear. According to him, what makes Christianity unique is belief in Christ, which has been consistently advocated by the Bible and throughout the history of the church. Therefore the New Theology, with its insistence on belief in God in the same way that Jesus believed in God, missed the essence of Christianity.

To prove his point, Kozaki discussed the origin of Christianity, dealing with the question of "Jesus or Paul," as raised by William Wrede and others. New Theology insisted that Pauline theology, which makes Jesus the object of faith, had nothing to do with Jesus' own teachings. Its advocates therefore called for a return to Jesus, abandoning Paul. Kozaki's view was that Pauline theology was a natural development of the gospel proclaimed by Jesus. This reflects his view that Christianity was capable of developing along the right lines through the guidance of the Holy Spirit.

Following Peter T. Forsyth, Kozaki divided current trends in Christianity into two groups: one that believes in Jesus, and one that believes in God, as Jesus did. The difference between them derives from their different ideas of sin, which in turn are based on their ideas of God. New Theology, which is based on a pantheistic immanentism and which teaches an optimistic view of man, cannot satisfy those people who have had the experience of examining themselves critically before God. Another distinction results from their different emphases. The first emphasizes the need for a dramatic leap into repentance and a new life; the second emphasizes the development of self-awareness and deeper understanding. The latter is represented by New Theology, and does not differ from the enlightenment (Kensho) of Buddhism or ultimate knowledge (Kakubutsu chishi) of Confucianism. A further distinction that Kozaki drew between the groups was between faith and knowledge, and between salvation by one's own efforts and salvation from without. He also tried to prove the errors in New Theology by reference to church history. In recent history, groups such as Socinians, Unitarians, and those American Congregationalists who had embraced the ideas of liberal theology had enjoyed short-term popularity because of the freshness of their ideas, but had then decreased in numbers. On the other hand, those denominations that had maintained orthodox ideas, which appeared narrow-minded to some and seemed to be contradicted by modern academic theories as well as by common sense, had grown in numbers. The reason was that they were rooted in evangelism and carried on evangelical activities vigorously.

In spite of his criticisms of New Theology, Kozaki did not deny the free spirit of inquiry among its adherents. He described his own position as "progressive evangelicalism," and explained it as follows:

> What I call "progressive evangelicalism" is the so-called modern Christianity, which makes full use of free studies, and recognizes the application of modern scientific thought and the laws of the study of history to religious questions. I do not differ from the scholars of New Theology in the process and direction of their faith and thought, but only in their results. I do not believe in God and Christ and in his redemption because of the infallibility of the Bible. I came to this belief as the result of studying the Bible and the history of Christianity objectively, at the same time becoming aware of my own faith.

New Theology tried to make human reason the basis of understanding Christianity, going so far as to exclude revelation. Although Kozaki also made human reason the basis of cognition, he believed that the final criterion of Christianity was the human reason that accepted revelation; in other words, "reason sanctified by the Holy Spirit," or the judgment of those who had had a faith-experience of salvation through the gospel.

What value, then, can be given to Kozaki's position? He lived in a period of theological conflict between liberalism and fundamentalism, surrounded by advocates and sympathizers of the New Theology. Taking a middle position, he rejected on the one hand the infallibility of the Bible, and on the other hand rational interpretation of the Bible. He advocated the evangelicalism that believed in Jesus Christ and his salvation, transcending the conflict between liberalism and fundamentalism. He put this forward as the essence of Christianity which was to be found throughout the Bible and the history of the church, at the same time employing modern ways of thinking and academic disciplines.

How far did Kozaki succeed in all of this? As the passage quoted above shows, he claimed that he made full use of the results of modern historical studies. However, we may justifiably ask how far the results of historical criticism of the Gospels are reflected in his biblical interpretation of the problem of the historical Jesus and the Jesus of faith. His conclusions were based more on common sense. He alleged that liberalism must be wrong because its supporters were decreasing in number, while the supporters of orthodoxy were increasing, but this is hardly a convincing argument. The question of truth or falsehood cannot be judged in this way. Furthermore, if "reason sanctified by the Holy Spirit" is the final criterion of truth, as he said, then the Bible and the church's historical tradition may be given equal weight, making no distinction between the Bible and the creeds.

In the name of progressive evangelicalism, Kozaki introduced Confucian ideas on government and the theory of evolution into Christianity. As a result, the tension inherent in the relationship between reason and revelation gradually faded away, and an easy combination of both came into being. This is why Kozaki's theology failed to provide a point of view from which to criticize the behavior of the imperial state of modern Japan.

Kanzo Uchimura's Conception of the Non-church (Mu-Kyokai)

When Kanzo Uchimura returned from his studies in America in 1888, he taught in various Christian schools and a state college and also worked as a journalist before finally becoming an independent evangelist. For the next forty years his life was full of turmoil. Because of his unique personality and strong sense of mission, he clashed with the violent stream of modern Japan.

Uchimura's earnest seeking for a way to believe in Christ as a Japanese soon led to a clash with missionaries and to his estrangement from the established churches. In 1900 he held a meeting with those people who shared his concerns and were in sympathy with him. Participants at the meeting, who came from various parts of Japan, then started up their own meetings wherever they lived. In order to promote evangelism and fellowship with these people, Uchimura began to publish a monthly journal, *The Study of the Bible.* At the same time he held meetings every Sunday in his own home, where he delivered lectures. He came to regard the community that grew out of these meetings as the "Mu-kyokai," or Non-church. The circulation of the journal increased, as did the size of the meeting, and many new groups were formed. After his death, his followers continued his methods of evangelism, and the Non-church Movement continues to the present day.

After World War II, Emil Brunner visited Japan in 1949 and remained as a visiting professor at the International Christian University from 1953 to 1955, at the same time engaging in evangelism and lecturing on theology in many parts of the country. According to Brunner, the essence of the church is the community of Christ, which is a personal fellowship of the Holy Spirit. In the course of history, however, the church has become a legal institution as the product of a process of development, change, or regression of the *ecclesia* of the New Testament (*Das Mißverständnis der Kirche,* 1951). Brunner was naturally interested in the Non-church Movement, which seemed to advocate ideas similar to his own; and he tried to act as a bridge between the church and the Non-church. After his return to Switzerland, he wrote several articles in praise of Uchimura and the Non-church Movement.

Carlo Caldarola, an American religious sociologist, also wrote a book entitled *Christianity: The Japanese Way,* in 1979. After studying Uchimura and other leaders of the Non-church and analyzing its present situation by means of a sociological survey, he came to the conclusion that the Non-church is one of the best examples of the indigenization of Christianity in Japan. Since there are several other books about Uchimura available in English, his conception of the Non-church has become better known in the Western world.

It must be said at the outset that Uchimura did not reject the idea of the church, nor neglect it, nor say that it was useless. In fact, he positively affirmed what he regarded as the essence of the church and recognized the need for it. However, he did regard the church of his own time as having departed from that essence; and thus he argued the need for the Non-church to counter this development.

According to his article "Ekklesia" (*The Study of the Bible,* 1910, No. 5), the original meaning of *ekklesia* is different from that of *kuriakon,* the word from which "church" is ultimately derived, which means "house of the Lord." *Ekklesia* means "congregation" or "meeting." According to the Gospels, Christ tried to "create a unique spiritual congregation, not on the basis of rule or law, but on the basis of that faith which is grounded in love, and which is derived from the freely taken decision to believe in Jesus as the Christ." Christ did not seek to "establish a church which modelled itself upon a government in its forms," but a "brotherly community like a family." He went on to write:

> In the so-called church, there are bishops, elders, theologians, constitutions and creeds. It is a kind of government or political party, which tries to expand its power and save the people, not by faith, but by public opinion. Though it is called the Church, it is not the Church built by Christ. In contrast to this kind of Church, we openly insist on the Non-church. (*The Study of the Bible*, 1921, No. 11)

It must be admitted that Uchimura does not seem to have rejected laws or constitutions in principle. According to his article "Institution and Life" (*The Study of the Bible*, 1916, No. 4), life is more than institutions. It cannot be born, moved, or bound according to rule. Unlike institutions, life is fresh and free. Therefore, those people who regard institutions as important regard life as dangerous. In contrast to these people, those who put life and faith first and institutions second argue in their turn that institutions are merely the product of faith. These latter people gave birth to Non-churchism. In other words, Uchimura maintains that in principle institutions may be created as the products of faith, but that in reality they turn out to be in conflict with life and lead to stagnation. In fact, the fellowship of believers in Christ with their spiritual life are in sharp conflict with the institutional church with its legal structures. As long as this conflict exists, it is necessary to maintain the Non-church.

Since Uchimura's Non-churchism was based on arguments derived from the contemporary situation, its emphases could change with changing circumstances. This can be seen in his views on the sacraments. When he was a student at Sapporo, he founded the Sapporo Independent Church; and he continued to be a member of it, except for a short period. Since the church was divided over the question of whether to abolish baptism and holy communion, they sought Uchimura's opinion. He gave his answer in his article "On Abolishing Baptism and Holy Communion" (*The Study of the Bible*, 1901, No. 2):

The administration of the sacraments may be beneficial for nurturing faith, but nobody can say that participation in them is essential for salvation. One cannot be saved by deeds (i.e., participation in rites), but by faith. One must receive the baptism of the Spirit, not of water. Only those who have been saved by Christ know the significance of the sacraments. If I were asked to choose one of them, either faith in Jesus Christ, or the administration of the sacraments, I would choose the former. In order to clarify the power of the Spirit through faith, why don't you abolish baptism and holy communion at this time? The mission of the Sapporo Independent Church is to proclaim the Gospel.

These views were expressed at the time when Uchimura was beginning to promote Non-churchism. At this time he was hostile towards the sacraments, contrasting evangelical faith and church rituals. However, about ten years later he wrote "Baptism and Holy Communion" (*The Study of the Bible*, 1912, No. 9). Just before writing this article, his beloved daughter Ruth had died from an illness. As her death approached, her faith increased, and she received holy communion with her parents for the only time in her life. She passed away a few hours later. Uchimura described this scene very emotionally in "Blessed Illness" (*The Study of the Bible*, 1912, No. 2). The article on the sacraments seems to have been written in memory of her.

In this article he writes, as he did earlier, that sacraments cannot save human souls. However, sacraments *(sacramenta)*, he says, are signs *(notae)* of holy things, and they are visible expressions of the invisible grace of God. Baptism is "a sign of the faith of believers concerning the death and resurrection of Christ," and an expression of the "revolutionary" faith by which one dies to sin and is born anew in Christ. Holy communion is a sign that reminds one of Christ's suffering and is a means of receiving his spiritual life. The spiritual life of believers cannot be sustained by the ritual of holy communion. Real participation in holy communion is reading the Bible, which conveys the word of God in a spirit of piety. However, he says that if one participates in holy communion with faith, then faith, hope, and love, which cannot be communicated by words, would be communicated among the participants. Perhaps he was here remembering the holy communion celebrated at the deathbed of his daughter. He was thinking of the sacraments as a sign of faith, transcending the dimension of conflict between faith and ritual.

Let us now examine the place which Non-churchism held in Uchimura's thoughts and actions. Two of his articles may be mentioned in this connection. The first is the often quoted article "The Conception of the Non-church" (*Non-Church*, 1901, No. 3), which he wrote around 1900, the time when he began to put forward Non-churchism specifically. He explains the Non-church in various ways. For example, he says that the Non-church does not ignore nor try to destroy the church, but is a church for people who have no institutional church, like those who have no money, parents, or house. The true church is Non-church. In heaven there are no clergy or sacraments. The Non-church tells the world what the community in the coming kingdom of God will be like. However, he says that we need the church as long as we are in this world. He describes the image of this church as follows:

> It is the universe created by God. It is nature. This is the church of the Non-church believers in this world. Its ceiling is the blue sky, and it is inlaid with stars. Its floor is green fields. Its carpets are colourful flowers. Its musical instruments are pine trees. Its musicians are the birds of the forest. Its pulpit is the top of a mountain, and its preacher is God Himself. This is the church that belongs to us, the believers of Non-church. The Non-church is indeed a church. Only those who have no church have the best church.

Uchimura does not talk about a concrete form of the Non-church at all. However, the image of the church that the Non-church is seeking and the conception upon which his idea of the Non-church is based are clear. His conception is that the Non-church is not artificial, but natural. This conception is a remarkable reflection of one aspect of the Japanese view of nature. Since ancient times, the Japanese have felt close to nature and have believed that they are able to obtain satisfaction in life through union with nature. From this point of view, human society is a world of chaos and madness, full of deception and artificiality. It thus became one of the earnest prayers of the Japanese to escape from this world in order to be embraced by nature. This way of thinking draws a distinction between nature and human artificiality and leads to patterns of living intended to introduce nature into daily life. If one compares an oil painting with a black-and-white drawing, a flower garden with a bare courtyard, a painted house with a plain wooden house, then one can see how different Japanese ways of thought are from Western ones.

As a Japanese, Uchimura shared this way of thinking. For him the laws, institutions, and organizations of the Western churches and denominations were artificial and unnatural. The church of God and Christ, he came to think, should be much more simple, pure, and naive. Ideas such as these were connected to his way of interpreting the Bible. He did not accept traditional doctrines and creeds as criteria. He read the Bible with a Japanese heart. One of the results of this was his view of the *ekklesia* described above. In this connection, he rejected both the Roman Catholic Church and the Protestant denominations in the following words:

> The Gospel in which I believe, is: Jesus Christ and him crucified. I protest against any doctrine or set of doctrines which go beyond, or do not come up to, this simplest of all doctrines. Protestantism, as I understand it, is Christ *versus* human ingenuity, faith *versus* churches. It is simplicity arrayed against complexity, living organisms against dead organizations. (*Protestantism*, 1916, No. 5)

This leads him to say that should his own Non-church depart from the principles of Protestantism, he would protest. Here one can see a beautifully drawn ellipse in which Christian faith and the Japanese consciousness of beauty are the two axes.

For a long time, Uchimura had believed that when a true Japanese believed in Christ, true Japanese Christianity would be born. This Christianity would be neither an imitation of Western Christianity nor "Japanized" Christianity. Just as Christianity had developed a unique tradition in the West, so an independent and unique form of Christianity should be born in Japan. Non-church Christianity, Uchimura believed, might prove to be such a Christianity.

The last article that he wrote in 1930 was published posthumously. The following is an excerpt from it:

> My Non-Churchism was not an "ism" for the sake of an "ism." It was an "ism" for faith. It was a conviction, arising from the assertion that one cannot be saved by works, but only by faith. . . . It [my Non-

Churchism] was not an "ism" to attack the Church. It was an "ism"
for advocating faith. Faith in the Cross comes first, and leads to
Non-Churchism. The Cross is the first "ism," and Non-Churchism
the second or third. The reason why I sometimes strongly attacked
the Church was that there were some people whose faith was not in
accordance with the truth of the Gospel. . . . In order to clarify my
position, I must say this: I am not part of the Non-Churchism
fashionable today. I have no desire to attack the weak Church of
today. I will proclaim the Gospel of the Cross more loudly in the
short time remaining to me. If necessary, this Gospel will destroy the
Church and restore it. I am a Non-Churchist to such an extent that
I am indifferent to the problems of the Church. I want to be a
Non-Churchist, who rejects all churches called churches, and all
"isms" called "isms." (*Gesammelte Werke* 32, pp. 347f.)

Uchimura wrote this partly in response to the ideas of one of his
disciples. Among the most capable of these was Toraji Tsukamoto
(1885-1973). For Tsukamoto, the faith of the church and the faith of
the Non-church were incompatible. Since the church insists that "unless one goes to church, one cannot be saved," argued Tsukamoto, the
Non-church should assert that "there is salvation outside the Church."
He went so far as to say:

If my belief is wrong and the Church's belief is right, namely, if it
is impossible to be saved by faith alone, my salvation is hopeless,
and the reason why I believe in Christ will have disappeared.

In reply to this, Uchimura advised Tsukamoto that one should not
think of the church and the Non-church in terms of either/or. Instead,
it was necessary to be friendly to both and to guide them. Uchimura's
last article was written to express his acute disagreement with
Tsukamoto, alleging that his views were "an 'ism' for an 'ism's' sake," and
intended to attack the church. He disassociated himself from such Non-
churchism. He described himself again as an independent *evangelist*.
This did not mean, however, that he had abandoned Non-churchism,
since for him his concept of the Non-church was the inevitable conclusion of his faith. Even in his final years, however, he repeatedly said that
at the heart of the church's problems was whether the present church

was really the church of Christ or not. In fact, he remained an *independent* evangelist until his death.

The question still remains as to whether or not Uchimura constructed his idea of the Non-church on a theological basis. As already described, he drew a sharp distinction between the church as a fellowship of believers and the church as an institution, between evangelical faith and church ritual. In other words, he understood the dual nature of the church, and saw these distinctions as contradictions. However, this point of view does not necessarily seem to be consistent with his view of the sacraments. Furthermore, he incorporated Japanese ways of thinking into his concept of the Non-church without subjecting them to a full theological examination. In the last resort, his own Non-churchism was the expression of a critical spirit directed toward the church as it existed then (including the Non-church). He wanted above all to be a free and original Japanese Christian.

CHAPTER 2

The Second Generation

TOSHIO SATO

Historical Survey (1907-1945)

The Rise of Theological Studies

AFTER 1907 theological studies in Japan finally began to be undertaken by Japanese themselves. The same can also be said of other fields of academic studies. For example, until this period philosophy had been taught mainly by foreigners like Fenollosa, Cooper, Busse, Koebel, and others at Tokyo Imperial University. After 1907, however, Japanese began to play the main role in teaching, and they also began to produce their own academic works. Similarly, after 1907 academic works in theology written by disciples and the younger members of the first generation leaders (Kanzo Uchimura, Masahisa Uemura, Danjo Ebina, and Hiromichi Kozaki) began to appear. Examples of these works are Tokumaro Tominaga's *New Interpretation of Christianity* (1909); En Kashiwai's *Short History of Christianity* (1909); Tsutomu Murata's *History of the Reformation* (1909); Mizutaro Takagi's *Great Dictionary of Christianity* (1911); and Toshimichi Imai's *Old Testament Theology* (1911).

The Origin of Christianity (1908) by Seiichi Hatano (1877-1950) is, however, the most remarkable work published in this period. This work served as the starting point for many other academic works that appeared during the period. Hatano studied at Tokyo Imperial University (which was founded in 1877 as the first national university, and remained the only one until 1897), and was baptized by Masahisa Uemura.

43

Deeply influenced by Raphael von Koeber, a Russian-German, he learned a philological approach to the classics of philosophy. His doctoral thesis was *A Study of Spinoza*, written in German. A few years before this, his first book, *The Outline of the History of Western Philosophy*, had been published. Though it was the work of a twenty-four year old, it was an outstanding achievement in the world of what was still at that time immature Japanese philosophy.

Hatano went to Germany in 1904 and studied there for two years. In Berlin he attended the lectures of Otto Pfleiderer and Adolf von Harnack; in Heidelberg he learned about the philosophy of the Badische Schule through Wilhelm Windelband. In theology he was attracted by the lectures of Johannes Weiss, Ernst Troeltsch, and Adolf Deissmann. As soon as he returned to Japan in 1906, he began to teach Primitive Christianity at Tokyo Imperial University as a part-time lecturer. His book *The Origin of Christianity*, published two years later, was based upon these lectures. In his preface he says:

> If you want to study the history of Christianity today, you have to study in the German academic world. Needless to say, I owe a great deal to its great scholars, especially Bousset, Dobschütz, Harnack, H. J. Holtzmann, Jülicher, Knobb, Pfleiderer, J. Weiss, Weizäcker, Wernle, Wrede and Zahn.

From this one can see how willingly and enthusiastically Hatano tried to absorb and digest the fruits of German scholarship. Although he was most influenced by the Religionsgeschichte Schule, which was then at its peak, he also learned from other schools, as the names listed above indicate. *The Origin of Christianity* was the result of these studies in Germany. It is also worth mentioning that Hatano was not an ordained minister, but a layman, who had not studied at a theological school. His academic interest was thus aroused at a secular university. His Christian studies were the personal application of the scholarship of the Tokyo Imperial University, a state university. This was the way that Christian studies came to be recognized in the Japanese academic world.

After Hatano, several students followed the same path, graduating from Tokyo University and taking up the academic study of Christianity without attending a theological school. Even today at Tokyo University (the name adopted by Tokyo Imperial University after World War II), which has no theological faculty, it is possible to undertake the academic study of Christianity to a certain extent, especially the philological and historical study of the New Testament. At the same time, however, one has to study Christianity by oneself along with the academic disciplines acquired at the state university. Some of the more fortunate students have been able to go to Germany to further their studies.

Ken Ishihara (1882-1976) was among those who specialized in the history of Christianity. He studied philosophy at the Tokyo Imperial University and came under the influence of Hatano, who was senior to him. Later, after having studied in Germany under Hans von Schubert, he taught at Tokyo Imperial University as professor of ancient and medieval history and Western philosophy. However, he devoted himself to the study of the history of Christianity and the history of Christian thought and became a pioneer in Japan in the study of Christian history.

Shigehiko Sato (1887-1935), who was baptized by Danjo Ebina, studied at Tokyo and Kyoto Imperial Universities. While doing postgraduate work in Tokyo, he was taught by Masahisa Uemura at the Tokyo Theological Seminary, which Uemura had founded. He then went to Germany and studied in Berlin and Tübingen. Under Karl Holl's guidance, he devoted himself to the study of Luther. After his return, he was recognized as an authority in Luther studies in Japan.

Teruo Soyano (1889-1927), who was baptized by Uemura, studied philosophy at Tokyo Imperial University. After teaching at Fukuoka Higher School, a high school specializing in the humanities, he was invited to teach philosophy and theology at Tokyo Theological Seminary by Tokutaro Takakura, who had succeeded Uemura as its president. Though he died rather young, Soyano devoted himself in his later years to the study of St. Augustine.

Seigo Yamaya (1889-1982) studied law at Tokyo Imperial University and became a government official. However, because he wanted to study Christianity, especially the New Testament, he taught law in higher schools and pursued biblical studies on his own. After receiving a doctorate from Kyoto Imperial University for his work on St. Paul, he taught Primitive Christianity at the same university.

All four of these scholars, like Hatano, studied at Tokyo Imperial University, and none of them attended a theological school in order to be ordained. Although Sato and Yamaya entered the ministry later, the other two remained laymen. While two of them went to Germany to study, most of them undertook their own studies by themselves. It is interesting to note that all of them, including Hatano, were influenced by Uemura. This means that Uemura trained not only ministers, but also scholars who later pursued academic studies in Christianity. Another feature worth mentioning is that it was through these scholars that German theological studies were introduced into the Japanese Christian world. Before this time, Japanese Protestant churches had learned their theology mainly through American missionaries. The exception was liberal Christianity, which was introduced by Spinner, a German missionary from the Allgemeiner Evangelisch-Protestantischer Missionsverein in 1885.

The introduction of German scholarship, which certainly raised the level of theological studies in Japan, was not unrelated to the new educational policy of the government, which decided around 1887 to follow the German model. After this, German became the predominant foreign language in state universities, while English remained the main foreign language in Christian schools. As a result, most of the theological schools sent their graduates to America for further training in order to become professors of theology, while Christians who graduated from state universities went to Germany to study Christianity, bringing back the fruits of German academic theology. An exception to this rule was the Tokyo Theological Seminary (Tokyo Shingakusha), which was founded by Uemura, not by American missionaries. Uemura encouraged students to study British theology and the German language rather than American theology. Furthermore, as many of the graduates from the state university gathered at Uemura's church, he influenced many lay scholars who studied German theology.

Of course, these were not the only scholars who produced academic Christian work in this period. There were graduates from other theological schools in Japan who went to America to study and who came back to teach and to pursue further studies. For example, there were professors like Masumi Hino (1874-1943) from the Doshisha School of Theology, who wrote the first book on the history of Christian doctrine; Zenda Watanabe (1885-1978) from the Meiji Gakuin School of Theology, whose field of study was the Old Testament, and who later went to Germany to study; Kyoji Tominomori (1887-1954), a New Testament

46

scholar from Doshisha; and Setsuji Otsuka (1887-1977), active in Christian ethics, also from Doshisha. Although some of these will be discussed later, most of them studied in America in their youth, and also acquired a knowledge of German, adapting to the currents in Japanese academic life.

Let us now return to Hatano and look at his development in later years, for he was the first to introduce German academic work into Japan. In 1917 he was appointed professor at Kyoto Imperial University, where he taught the philosophy of religion. Thereafter, he employed all his powers in the construction of a coherent system of thought. In 1920 he published *The Essence and the Basic Problems of the Philosophy of Religion*. At this stage his own views were not yet firmly established, for his approach to the problem of the essence of religion was taken from Schleiermacher's criticism, as advocated by Troeltsch. As the trend in German academia moved away from neo-Kantian criticism to the psychology and phenomenology of religion, Hatano also moved in the same direction. In his *Introduction to the Philosophy of Religion* (1940), he wrote: "The philosophy of religion must be the theoretical retrospection of religious experience and the reflective self-understanding of it." This was in accordance with Wobbermin's methodology of religious psychology, as Hatano acknowledged in a letter to Enkichi Kan. Hatano's earlier *Philosophy of Religion* (1935) and his later *Time and Eternity* (1943) were both written on the basis of this methodological position. Together these three books form a trilogy.

Hatano's philosophical position can be summed up in one word: *personalism*. However, his form of personalism, in contrast with other forms, has a unique characteristic. He divides life into three stages. The first stage is "natural life," in which one keeps one's own reality, destroying the reality of others and reducing it to things. The second stage is "cultural life," in which the reality of the other withdraws from the place of the other, while the object as ideal being takes its place, becoming a neutral zone to be contemplated by the subject. (In philosophical terms this is idealism.) The third stage is "religious life," which is not a relation between I and thing, but a personal relation with God, as you and I. The basis of this personal community is love. Hatano's last work, *Time and Eternity*, which contains his most mature thought, is an application of his basic ideas of life in terms of time and eternity in a form of future development.

Evangelical Christianity

Tokutaro Takakura (1885-1934) was also a disciple of Uemura. Although he entered Tokyo Imperial University to study law, he transferred to Uemura's Tokyo Theological Seminary. After graduation, he immediately became a minister, serving the churches in Kyoto and Sapporo, where he continued to study theology. In 1918 he was appointed professor at Tokyo Theological Seminary, and in 1921 he went to Great Britain to study. At first he went to Scotland and studied under H. R. Mackintosh and W. Paterson at New College, Edinburgh. He was especially influenced by the latter's theology, which he called "Calvinistic evangelism." After nine months in Edinburgh, he was invited by Ken Ishihara to travel to Germany, and he observed the world of theology there. Returning to England, he entered Mansfield College, Oxford, where he devoted himself to reading Troeltsch, von Hügel, and Forsyth. The fact that he simultaneously read the works of these theologians and philosophers of religion, whose backgrounds were so different, shows the wide range of the theological interests of the young Takakura. He then moved to Cambridge, where he was impressed by John Oman.

In 1924 Takakura came back to Japan and began to teach at Tokyo Theological Seminary, becoming its president after the death of Uemura. Besides his teaching work, he founded the Toyama Church. This church, which later became the Shinanomachi Church, included among its members Hatano, Ishihara, Soyano, and Yamaya, who later became its minister. Takakura also undertook evangelical work, and it was during this period that his so-called evangelical Christianity took shape. Among the three theologians and philosophers of religion mentioned above, he chose to study Forsyth in particular, and advocated his own unique theological position.

Evangelical Christianity (1924) was Takakura's most representative work. This work provided a good summary of his theology and became a widely read bestseller. Before the publication of this book, a trilogy of his earlier works showed the development of his theological thinking: *Kingdom of Grace* (1921), *Grace and Faithfulness* (1921), and *Grace and Calling* (1925).

The subject of his graduation thesis at Tokyo Theological Seminary was Schleiermacher, and one can still hear echoes of this in his first published work, *Kingdom of Grace*. Gradually, however, his faith in the

Atonement developed, and by the time of *Grace and Faithfulness,* he had largely moved to his position of evangelical Christianity. He was, however, not satisfied with this stage. In his third book, *Grace and Calling,* which was a collection of his sermons delivered at the Toyama Church, his standpoint of evangelical faith and Christianity was presented clearly and precisely. Accordingly, one can say that his evangelical faith was established either by the end of 1924 or at the beginning of 1925.

What, then, are his evangelical faith and Christianity all about? He had received them from his teacher, Masahisa Uemura. Although Uemura was a man of profound learning and culture, his Christianity was evangelical, and he described it as such. At the root of Uemura's evangelical Christianity were the missionaries from America, such as Brown, Hepburn, Ballagh, and others from whom he learned. They were all supporters of the World Evangelical Alliance, founded in Great Britain in the nineteenth century. The starting point of the first Japanese church founded in Yokohama by Uemura and others was the New Year's prayer meeting of the World Evangelical Alliance. The Alliance had as its targets "Romanism" and High Church Anglicanism, and was characterized by the *Erweckungsbewegung,* which was supported by people of missionary spirit and passion. Uemura learned about evangelical Christianity from those American missionaries, and deepened his understanding of Christianity by studying the books of British theologians such as Forsyth and Denney. Takakura inherited this kind of Christianity from Uemura, and deepened and refined it by the culture acquired at Tokyo Imperial University and by what he had learned from theologians in Great Britain.

What, then, is the content of Takakura's evangelical Christianity? He was known for introducing Calvin into Japan, as Sato introduced Luther. Although it is true that Calvin's influence upon his faith is strong, Takakura did not like to be labeled a Calvinist, saying, "The main point that I want to insist on is to recognize and experience Christianity as the religion of the Bible, and to make it appeal to others." The religion of the Bible means Christianity, as begun by the Prophets, continued into the New Testament, and made alive by the Reformers. This is what he called evangelical Christianity. From this point of view, Catholicism and modern liberal and cultural Christianity are nothing but an amalgam of biblical religion and pagan elements.

49

Thus, Takakura's theological thinking was very close to that of Forsyth. Just as Forsyth was known after World War II as "the Barthian before Barth," Takakura engaged in theological fighting similar to Forsyth's and Barth's. In fact, he fought against contemporary liberal theology, humanistic Christianity, and Social Christianity. It was a matter of course that he sympathized with dialectical theology when it was introduced, and that many of his disciples were influenced by it. In terms of the history of theology, he prepared the way for dialectical theology, which was to exercise a great influence upon theology in Japan.

Social Christianity

The beginning of Christian socialism in Japan is to be found in the Meiji period. During this period, the importance of Christian socialism within the whole socialist movement in Japan was great. The majority of socialists were Christian, although after the Taisho period materialistic socialism predominated.

The socialist movement of the Meiji period fell into obscurity because of a case of high treason — an attempted assassination of the Emperor Meiji in 1918, which is alleged to have been a frame-up by the government. However, at the start of the Taisho period, signs of revival began to appear. Toyohiko Kagawa (1888-1960) led the labor movement in Japan at that time. Although he moved from work in the slums into the labor movement, the basis of his philosophy can be said to be Christian socialism. He could not, therefore, get along with the Marxist labor movement, which was then coming to the fore. Though he was at first on the extreme left of the labor movement, he was gradually pushed to the extreme right. Then he committed himself to the cooperative movement and later to the nationwide evangelistic movement called The Kingdom of God.

The beginning of the Showa period saw the rise of a movement of Social Christianity. Unlike the Christian socialism of the Meiji and Taisho periods, which was a movement directed towards those outside the church, Social Christianity was rather a criticism directed within. Its main thrust was to propose that a socialized Christianity take precedence over individualistic Christianity.

Christian students were the main supporters of this movement. At the beginning of the Showa period, the Student Christian Movement (SCM) grew out of the Young Men's Christian Association (YMCA). However, since many people thought that SCM stood for Social Christian Movement, it was very much influenced by the thinking of Social Christianity, and became its spearhead. Its leaders were Shigeru Nakajima (1888-1946), Enkichi Kan (1895-1972), and Yonetaro Kimura (1889-1949), among others.

Nakajima was the leading ideologue of the movement. He had studied law at Tokyo Imperial University, meanwhile attending the Hongo Church of Danjo Ebina. Then, as professor, he taught law at Doshina University and later at Kansei Gakuin University. He became a central figure of a social Christian movement that started before SCM and continued even after its collapse. In 1931 at the Kyoto YMCA he organized the Kansai (Western area) Alliance of Social Christianity, which in 1933 was reorganized into the National Alliance of Social Christianity, and he published a magazine, *Social Christianity*.

Because Nakajima used the expression "redemptive love," he seemed to have been influenced by Kagawa, whom he respected. There is, however, no indication that he was influenced by the Social Gospel of America, though he certainly knew about it. He had his own social philosophy upon which he insisted. He wrote several books on the subject of Social Christianity. *God and Community* (1929) was his starting point. Then he published *Social Christianity and the New Experience of God* (1931) and *The Essence of Social Christianity: The Religion of Redemptive Love* (1937). His basic point of view is consistent, and these books are merely variations upon it. He starts from the concept of the kingdom of God, which he interprets as the "community of God." According to Nakajima, "community" is different from "association." Nation, church, the League of Nations, labor unions, and companies are associations that each have a certain purpose, organization, constitution, and regulations, along with members' rights and duties. On the other hand, community is basically a relationship between persons, an unorganizational voluntary community which is the basis of all associations, and includes all of them. Nakajima calls this the community of union and community of solidarity. Community progresses not through the class struggle, as Marxism insists, but by an increase in personal union and the development of solidarity.

51

He calls this progress "communization" and says that love makes the community progress in communization. At the apex of community progress he sees the kingdom of God, the highest realization of the community of union.

Nakajima's Social Christianity is more *religiös-sozial* than *christlich-sozial*, to use the German terms. However, he is obviously critical of Marxism, whereas the *religiös-sozial* values Marxism highly. He therefore argues for Social Christianity from the basis of his unique social philosophy. It should not be overlooked that his theory of social progress towards union is combined with his developmental view of history. According to him, the history of mankind starts with primitive society, proceeds to the medieval period of feudal military authoritarianism, then to the age of nationalistic constitutional capitalism, and is now arriving at the age of international socialism. The present society of international socialism rejects imperialistic struggles between nations, capitalist power relations, and the utilization of a monetary economy. It is going to become a great new community of mankind, and is, therefore, the society that is closest to the kingdom of God, the community of God. In this society, people eliminate egoistic motivation by the love of socialization; they change relationships based on power and struggle into relationships of cooperation and service; and they have the task of creating a community through increasing union and developing solidarity. Where this task is accomplished, there the kingdom of love is realized. What, then, is the relationship between the realization of the kingdom of God and Jesus Christ? For Nakajima, Christ is an abstract concept, another name for socialization (redemptive love), and for God himself who works in society. This means, therefore, that Christ is immanent, and works in every man and society, but is nothing more than a principle which has been working in heaven and earth and in the society of mankind since before the time of Jesus. However, because Jesus realized this Christ in the highest degree, Christ who appeared in Jesus has been called Jesus Christ. What, then, does he mean by salvation? Salvation is, of course, salvation from sin; and sin is action inspired by non-social egoistic motivation. Salvation is therefore to become socialized by Christ's love; the dying of the old self and the living of the new self, denying the non-social self and affirming the social self. Thus being saved is being moved by Jesus' love for socialization, getting rid of the life of sin and entering into the life of offering oneself to God, and engaging in the practice of the love of socialization with Jesus, cooperating towards the realization of the kingdom of God, praising the love of God.

It is worth noting that Nakajima does not exclude Paulinism, as the advocates of the Social Gospel did. According to him, insofar as Christianity is a religion of redemptive love and the gospel of the cross, no one can discard Paul's redemptive thought. The fundamental basis of Social Christianity is to practice redemptive love (love of socialization) with Jesus. He does not, however, accept "legalistic vicarious atonement," or "priestly sacrificial atonement." Paul's redemptive experience, he thinks, is that an inner social self discovers the highest manifestation of social self in Jesus and attains the liberation of the social self by absolute obedience to him. Atonement, then, should be interpreted not only passively, but actively. He emphasizes the practice of redemptive love. Though he often uses the word *atonement*, the question remains as to how accurately and concretely he thinks of it. In any case, it is characteristic of his Social Christianity that he does not exclude Paul.

Dialectical Theology

The starting point of dialectical theology is Karl Barth's *Römerbrief* (in English, *Commentary on Romans*), first published in 1919. In Japan the writings of Barth and Emil Brunner began to be read as early as 1925. At first they were introduced in newspaper and periodical articles, but they soon became so popular that translations and studies of them began to appear by 1930. In particular, Brunner's *Theology of Crisis,* translated by Gosaku Okada in 1931, was read not only in Christian circles but also much more widely.

The first study by a Japanese was Yoshitaka Kumano's *Introduction to Dialectical Theology* (1932). In the following year Hidenobu Kuwada's *Dialectical Theology* (1933) was published. Then Enkichi Kan wrote two books: *Religious Revival* (1934), which introduced dialectical theology, and *The Modern Philosophy of Religion* (1934), which faithfully introduced the thought of Brunner. Kumano was a student of Uemura, and evangelical in outlook from the beginning; while Kuwada, who studied in America, shifted from Ritschlian liberalism to dialectical theology. Kan, who was an ideologue of Social Christianity with Nakajima, also changed his views and became a supporter of dialectical theology. When they introduced this theology for the first time, they relied mainly on the writings of Brunner because they found it easier to understand dialectical theology through him. Even Takakura, who was older than Kumano, Kuwada, and Kan, and who had read dialectical theology earlier, used to say that Brunner was good, though Barth was dangerous.

However, as soon as Barth's *Kirkliche Dogmatik* (*Church Dogmatics*) began to be published in 1932, and Japanese theologians began to understand the characteristics of his theology, they turned to him rather than to Brunner. This tendency became decisive at the time of the controversy between Barth and Brunner on natural theology in 1934. Most theological scholars came down in favor of Barth, and since then they have been interested almost exclusively in him. This situation did not change even when Brunner came to Japan twice after World War II, in spite of his teaching at the International Christian University for two years as a visiting professor.

At the outset the study of Barth's theology was undertaken by groups in both Eastern and Western Japan. In the West (around Kyoto), a group was formed under Keiji Ashida, professor at the Doshisha School of Theology, to translate Barth's *Römerbrief*. Kagami Hashimoto, a central member of this group, was at that time a graduate student at Kyoto Imperial University. Though he wrote several articles on Barth, he devoted himself to studying Kierkegaard as well. Like Kierkegaard, he was very much interested in the monastic life. Tasuku Matsuo, another member of this group, studied German by himself, though because of illness he had had almost no formal education. Urged on by Egon Hessel, a missionary from Germany, he translated Barth's essays *Die Kirche und die Kultur, Rechtfertigung und Heiligung* and *Die Not der evangelischen Kirche*. Nobuo Harada, whose thesis at Doshisha was *The Anthropology of Karl Barth*, published a small book entitled *Exposition of Barth's Dogmatics* while ministering to a church. These three men died at comparatively young ages, but another member of this group who has lived to a much greater age is Yoshiki Shimizu. Although Shimizu was an ideologue of the SCM while he was a student before turning to Barth, he later became professor of theology at Kanto Gakuin University and published the two-volume *Protestant Theology*.

In the East (around Tokyo), a group at the Shinanomachi Church, founded by Takakura, was also active. Masatoshi Fukuda, who became minister of the Shinanomachi Church after Takakura's death in 1934, published a book entitled *Ordo Gratiae*. This was a collection of essays strongly influenced by Barth, especially Barth's christological standpoint. Takenosuke Miyamoto, also a member of this church, who graduated from the philosophy department of Tokyo Imperial University, examined the possibility of doing philosophy within Barth's frame of reference. Sakae Akaiwa, who became a prominent figure in journalism immediately after World War II and aroused controversy with his last book, *Exodus from Christianity*, then became a follower of Takakura and devoted himself to the study of Barth. Kano Yamamoto, influenced by Takakura and Barth, became a representative Barthian, consistent in his study and advocacy of Barth. Yoshio Yoshimura, who graduated from Tokyo Imperial University in philosophy, was interested in both Kierkegaard and Barth, and later translated Barth's *Commentary on Romans*. Yoshinori Matsutani, who studied philosophy, also moved into theology under Barth's inspiration, and wrote *Thinking of Theological Man* and *Introduction to the Doctrine of the Trinity*. Among translations of Barth, there was a joint project consisting of groups from Tokyo and Kyoto who published *Das Wort Gottes und die Theologie*. There was a journal called *Resurrection* in which Barth's influence was obvious, and to which the young Katsumi Takizawa contributed. Another journal deserving of mention is *The Word of the Cross*, published by Egon Hessel with the help of Kano Yamamoto. A series, *Theology of the Cross*, which contained translations of many of Barth's essays, played an important role in introducing his work. Nevertheless, there was no translation of Barth's main writings, nor had a standard study of his theology appeared before World War II. It was only after the war that *Church Dogmatics* was translated and that some of the younger generation wrote doctoral theses on Barth in Germany and Switzerland.

Why, then, did dialectical theology, and especially Barth's theology, make such a deep impression upon the Japanese Christian community? Many reasons might be given; however, the main reason was that Japanese Christian intellectuals of that time believed that in dialectical theology they had examined the depths of Christian thought. Although they were attracted by the Christianity taught by American missionaries, they were not aware of any other form of Christianity with an intellectual quality. It was the general view among the public that Buddhism was much more profound than Christianity. Moreover, most intellectuals had been influenced by German idealism since the middle of the Meiji period. So Christian intellectuals, who had been impressed by the depth of German idealism, were not satisfied with the Christian theology they had hitherto encountered, which was too shallow in its ways of thinking. When dialectical theology was introduced to Japan, it made a frontal attack upon German idealism. It is thus no wonder that Japanese Christians were very much attracted to it. Not only Christians, but many other intellectuals outside Christianity were attracted to it as well. For example, Kitaro Nishida, a leading philosopher, turned his attention to dialectical theology. His disciples, such as Tetsuo Watsuji and Kiyoshi Miki, who became a popular thinker, also discussed it. Consequently, dialectical theology came to hold a definite position in Japanese philosophical circles.

Why Japanese intellectuals were particularly attracted by Barth's theology is a question that remains to be answered in the future. But one reason, at least, is clear: the *radicalism* of Barth's theology. This radicalism can be a hindrance in a society where Christianity is deeply rooted. In such a society the common sense of Brunner's theology is more persuasive, and Barth's theology appears too radical. But in a society like Japan, where Christianity is not yet indigenized, commonsense theological thought is more likely to be despised. It is rather radicalism which is more interesting, attractive, and praiseworthy. This is the secret of dialectical theology, especially of Barth's theology, which has enjoyed an overwhelming influence in Japan.

Japanese Christianity

Just as a movement known as "Deutsche Christen" arose side by side with Nazism in Germany, "Japanese Christianity" arose with the growth of ultra-nationalism during wartime in Japan. There was, however, a great difference between Germany and Japan. The movement of the Deutsche Christen, closely connected to the Nazi government, led to the establishment of the "Bekennende Kirche" (Confessing Church), which fought against the movement. In Japan, however, Japanese Christianity was a minority group in Japanese society, and the mainstream churches were not so much influenced by it.

Nevertheless, there were already instances of this kind of movement in the Meiji period. During the nationalistic period, Michitomo Kanamori, for example, advocated a Japan-like Christianity; Danjo Ebina advocated a Shinto-like Christianity, uniting Japanese ethics and Christianity; and Tokio Yokoi insisted on a kind of Japanese Christianity that harmonized Confucianism and Christianity.

Japanese Christianity, which arose during the Showa period, advocated the following points:

1. Since *Mikuni* (kingdom of the emperor) and *Mikuni* (kingdom of God) are pronounced in the same way, serving the emperor and cooperation in Japan's advance into China serves the advancement of the kingdom of God.
2. The emperor and Christ are identical, otherwise Japanese would not believe in Christianity.
3. For the Japanese, if not for Westerners, Shintoist ancient writings such as Kojiki and Nihonshoki are the Old Testament.
4. Yahweh, the God of the Old Testament, and the god Amenominakanushinokami of Kojiki are identical.
5. As it is written in the Old Testament, especially in the Book of Isaiah, the mission of the Japanese is to restore Israel, and the war against China is part of that mission.

Most of those people who tried to combine Christianity with nationalism and patriotism ended by making certain changes in the content of the Christian faith. Some advocates cooperated positively with nationalism and war, while holding to the traditional Christian faith. Quoting, for instance, the words of Louis Pasteur, "Though there is no borderline in science, there is a borderline among scientists," they argued in favor of a Christianity supported by national consciousness, while recognizing the universal nature of the Christian faith.

To the question of why such a Japanese Christianity arose, the following answer may be given. Those Western ideas which Japan had imported were adopted only at a superficial level, whereas traditional thinking remained at a deeper level and would rise to the surface again when the right occasion occurred. As political scientist Masao Maruyama says in his book *The Thought of Japan* (1900), when a foreign thought is adopted into Japan, the past is never objectified and absorbed into the present. Traditional thoughts survive and accumulate. The past does not confront the present: it is pushed aside or disappears from consciousness and fades into "forgetfulness." The past, however, sometimes resurfaces as "memory." This happens to Christianity. Even if Christianity is accepted, traditional thought (ultra-nationalism) is not banished, but sinks to the bottom. Therefore, when the season for nationalism comes around, it resurfaces from the subconscious.

What kind of people were likely to turn to Japanese Christianity? The first group were those who had adopted liberal Christianity. Because they had no orthodox faith as a brake upon their ideas, they easily moved towards Japanese Christianity. Advocates of Japanese Christianity in the Meiji period, such as Kanamori, Ebina, and Yokoi, had become theologically liberal under the influence of the so-called New Theology. The second group were those associated with pietism. More concerned with the Bible and piety than with orthodox doctrine, they were sincere Christians. They believed that the Japanese should embrace the Japanese spirit, but that sinners are unable to do so. Only when one is justified by faith and sanctified can one become a master of the true Japanese spirit. In this way, they combined Christianity and the spirit of Japan.

The Development of Theological Studies

Biblical Studies

Zenda Watanabe

The representative figure in Old Testament studies of this period is Zenda Watanabe (1885-1978). Originally taught the verbal inspiration theory of the Bible at a Holiness Church, he was confronted with the question of "the principle of Biblical interpretation." He then went to America and took courses in biblical studies and the Old Testament at the Nazarene College in Pasadena, the Pacific School of Religion in Berkeley, and the University of California. When he returned as an Old Testament scholar, a modern approach to biblical studies had replaced his theory of verbal inspiration.

After teaching at Takinogawa Seigakuin Seminary and Doshisha School of Theology, Watanabe became a chaplain at Tokyo Woman's Christian College. At that time he published his first writings, three volumes of *The Theology of Old Testament Books* (1921-24), which showed his unusual ability as a writer. After that he continued to write books on the Old Testament until his last years. *Introduction to the Five Books of Moses* (1949) is a masterpiece, and *Before the Exodus* (1972), which described the Semitic world, is his last and great work.

As a theologian, Watanabe concentrated all his efforts on the doctrines of the Bible in order to answer the question of how the word of man becomes the word of God. His greatest concern, therefore, was with a theme of systematic theology. He wrote three books on the doctrine of the Bible: *Canonicity of the Bible* (1949), *Interpretation of the Bible* (1954), and *Theology of the Bible* (1963). Though these works were published after World War II, he had devoted himself to the doctrine of the Bible for ten years from 1935 onwards. Before this, Watanabe went to Germany to seek "the principles of biblical interpretation." On the recommendation of von Seeberg, he studied with Husserl in Freiburg. From Husserl he learned the phenomenological method, *zu der Sache selbst,* in which he found a key to replace historical critical study of the Bible. It was a method that corresponded with that of Barth and Brunner, who also tried to deal with historical criticism.

Of course, Watanabe does not completely deny the value of historical criticism. However, recognizing its limitations, he proposes a canonical, theological study of the Bible, as well as a philological, historical study. While the latter is concerned with the past (e.g., how the Bible was written), the former is concerned with the present (e.g., what is the Bible, and what is its essence?). According to Watanabe, even the philological, historical study of the Bible should be concerned solely with the dismantling of extraneous material and removing of later additions. It should also be concerned with the question of how materials were edited into the present form of the canon and how material was added later. Furthermore, the canonical, theological approach proposes that the Bible should be interpreted as canon, as the word of God; and it emphasizes its method as a way of entering into dialogue with the canon as "Thou." It means reading the Bible in the light of the "history of salvation."

Junichi Asano

Another scholar in the field of Old Testament study, Junichi Asano (1899-1982), was fifteen years younger than Watanabe. After first going into business, he studied at Tokyo Theological Seminary and the University of Edinburgh. His interest in the Old Testament was aroused by a professor of history at the college of commerce, and he was encouraged to study by his minister, Akira Mori. It was his teacher, Tokutaro Takakura, who especially recommended that he study the Old Testament, emphasizing its significance and the importance of the religion of the prophets. As a result, he went to Edinburgh to study under A. C. Welch.

After his return, although Asano taught as a lecturer at theological schools such as Tokyo, Nippon, and Aoyama, he wondered which profession he should choose as his main occupation, ministry or study. He finally decided to become a minister and founded the Mitake Church, though he continued to study as much as possible. Asano was typical of his theological generation, beginning to feel a conflict between being a minister-evangelist and an academic, unlike his teachers Uemura and Takakura. However, soon after his return, he published his first book, *A Study of the Prophets* (1931), with a preface by Takakura. Through his writings, such as *Interpretation of Some Psalms* (1933), *The Old Testament Bible* (1939), and *Some Problems of Old Testament Theology* (1941), he became known as a leading Old Testament scholar of his age.

During the war, however, Asano suffered a severe ordeal. He lost most of his property, in particular all of his books, through a fire caused by bombing, and he almost gave up his studies. Having recovered from his problems, he became a professor in the theological faculty of Aoyama Gakuin University, and put all his efforts into study and writing until the last years of his life, in spite of having undergone laparotomy twice. He then published his main work, *A Study of Israelite Prophets* (1955), as the first part of a trilogy. Although he was planning to write on the Wisdom Literature as the second part, he was fascinated by the Book of Job, perhaps because of his bitter experiences during the war, and published *A Study of the Book of Job* (1962) and *Commentary on the Book of Job* (4 vols., 1965-74). His forte was not philological study but theological thought, and his works as a whole remained pioneer works. His good writing and plain style can also be seen in later works, such as *The Book of Job* (1968), *The Psalms* (1972), and *Moses* (1980).

Seigo Yamaya

Needless to say, there were a considerable number of people who taught the New Testament at their theological schools and engaged in academic work.[1] Seigo Yamaya (1889-1982), however, deserves to be singled out for the number of his writings and the high academic standard that he achieved almost unaided. As already stated, Yamaya changed his career from that of government official to teacher in a state college, and he began to study the New Testament by himself. Unlike his contemporaries who came under Anglo-American influence, he studied German works on the New Testament under the influence of Hatano. Though he was familiar with the writings of the Religionsgeschichte Schule, because of Uemura's guidance, his own point of view was not radical but rather well balanced.

His most typical work, *The Theology of Paul* (1936), based upon his doctoral thesis, showed not only the influence of the Religionsgeschichte Schule but also his own views. He then undertook a work of exegesis, *The New Testament: A New Translation and Exegesis* (5 vols., 1930-48), which included 1 and 2 Thessalonians, Galatians, 1 and 2 Corinthians, Romans, Philippians, and Philemon.

After resigning from full-time teaching, he became the minister of Muromachi Church in Kyoto, and after the war of the Shinanomachi Church in Tokyo. For three years he served as a member of the committee working on the colloquial translation of the New Testament. Then he became professor at Tokyo Union Theological Seminary, continuing to write on the New Testament in works such as his *Origin of Christianity* (2 vols., 1957-58), a summary of his long years' study of Christian history; *Explanatory Bibliography of the New Testament* (1943), a kind of introduction to the New Testament; and *New Testament The-*

---

1. In the field of New Testament studies, other people should possibly be mentioned besides Yamaya, e.g., Toraji Tsukamoto and Kokichi Kurosaki. As these two will be discussed later in connection with the Mukyokai (Non-church) group, only Seigo Yamaya (1889-1982) will be dealt with in this section.

ology (1966), a summary of the theological thought of the New Testament. With these writings, Yamaya made a great contribution to New Testament studies, especially to studies of Paul in Japan. He was also known as the translator into Japanese of Harnack's *Das Wesen des Christentums,* and of Otto's *Das Heilige.*

Historical Theology

En Kashiwai (1870-1920) was the first Japanese to write a history of Christianity, and Masumi Hino (1874-1942) was the first to write a history of Christian doctrine. The former's *History of Christianity* was published posthumously in 1924, and the latter's *History of Christian Doctrine* appeared in 1917. Following them, four scholars should be mentioned for their contributions to the field of historical theology: Ken Ishihara, Tadakazu Uoki, Tetsutaro Ariga, and Shigehiko Sato.

Ken Ishihara

Ken Ishihara (1882-1976) was a pioneer in the field of the historical study of Christianity in Japan. As previously mentioned, he first studied history at Tokyo Imperial University, then changed to philosophy under Koeber. In Germany, however, he studied under von Schubert, the church historian. Although he taught the history of ancient and medieval Western philosophy at Tohoku Imperial University as a professor, Ishihara was by nature a historian, and he ended his long life as a historian of Christianity.

Although he published *The Philosophy of Religion* (1916) when he was young, he soon ordered that no more copies be printed. After that, he wrote a great many articles and books exclusively in the fields of the history of Christianity and the history of Christian thought. In this respect, a contrast can be drawn between Ishihara and his teacher, Seiichi Hatano, who concentrated on writing systematic works on the philosophy of religion in his later years, having earlier written on the history of thought with a philological background.

In his youth Ishihara had hoped to study the church fathers. His doctoral thesis at Tokyo Imperial University was on Clement of Alexandria. Then he wrote *Schleiermachers Reden über die Religion* (1922), a translation of the original, together with sixty pages of his own commentary and detailed explanation. During his teaching at Tohoku Imperial University, his interests expanded into various areas, such as Eckhart, Luther, and biblical studies. As he himself confessed, he had to venture out beyond his special subject. During this time he published *History of Christianity* (1934), which was one of a series of textbooks issued by Iwanami, the most prestigious Japanese publishing company. Although it was a short book, it was widely read for many years, for there were no other similar books in existence.

After retiring from Tohoku Imperial University, Ishihara became the president of Tokyo Women's Christian College, where he concerned himself with administration. He then returned to a quiet academic life teaching at Aoyama Gakuin University. By 1959 he had published twelve works on the Reformation, fifteen on the Roman Catholic Church, nine on New Testament theology and Primitive Theology, thirteen on Japanese and Oriental Christianity, and fifteen on other subjects. Among these works, his studies on the history of missions in the Orient were unique. He started work in this field at the suggestion of his teacher, von Schubert, who believed that attention to this subject was important for understanding Christianity in Japan. In his later years, Ishihara became a member of the Japanese Academy and received a Cultural Medal from the government. In addition to constantly revising his *History of Christianity*, he published his two last great works, *The Source of Christianity* (1972) and *The Development of Christianity* (1972).

Tadakazu Uoki

Tadakazu Uoki (1882-1954) graduated from Doshisha and went on to Union Theological Seminary in New York, where he studied under A. C. McGiffert, receiving an STM for his dissertation on Spener. He then studied in Marburg in Germany for half a year. After his return, he taught historical theology at Doshisha until his death. Although in his early years he wrote *History of Modern German Protestant Theological Thought* (1934), he concentrated throughout the whole of his life on Luther and Calvin.

Uoki's uniqueness as a historical theologian is his emphasis on Christian spiritual history, under the influence of Dilthey's *Geistesgeschichte*, rather than on the history of theology and the history of Christian thought. He attached importance to the living experience of the gospel as the "mother's womb, from which doctrine was born." His methodology for Christian spiritual history was, therefore, to describe that development. "Christian spiritual history," to use his own words, "is to study and describe the developments and changes in the understanding of the revelation and the experience of the Gospel, which originated in the Christian Church, as the group of believers, throughout the ages from the Primitive Church up to our own time."

Another of Uoki's methodologies was typology. According to him, the following types are to be found in Christian spiritual history: Greek, Latin, German, Anglo-Saxon, and Asian.[2] Although Uoki recognized differences between Luther and Calvin, he assigned both to the German type rather than establishing a separate French type. His *Christian Spiritual History: The Spirit of Calvin's Theology* (1948) was written from this point of view. He wrote several articles on Luther, but never managed to write a book on him. *The Spiritual Tradition of Japanese Christianity* (1941) deals in great detail with Japanese spirituality, which falls within Asian spirituality. He discusses how the Japanese, who were nurtured by Shintoism, Confucianism, and Buddhism, were changed by contact with the gospel of Christianity.

Tetsutaro Ariga

Like Uoki, Tetsutaro Ariga (1899-1977) graduated from Doshisha and went to America, where he studied at Chicago and Columbia Universities and Union Theological Seminary, from which he also received an STM. After his return, he began to teach, and continued teaching at Doshisha until he was invited to Kyoto University as professor of Christian studies in 1948.

In 1935 he went back to Union and wrote a thesis on Origen, thus becoming the first Japanese to receive the degree of Th.D. from that seminary. *A Study of Origen* (1943) was based upon his thesis. Previously, Ariga and Uoki had jointly written *An Outline of the History of Christian Thought* (1934), in which Ariga wrote the parts on the ancient and medieval world. After World War II he published a collection of articles under the title *Symbolical Theology* (1946), and in his last five years he

2. Uoki might have taken this typology from R. Seeberg.

wrote his main work, *The Problems of Ontology in Christian Thought* (1969).

As a church historian, Ariga followed Ishihara in the study of the church fathers. While Ishihara remained a pioneer in this field, Ariga took a step further in the study of Origen.

Although he limited himself to the study of ancient Christian thinkers, Ariga was concerned with the wider perspective of theology in general. He went to study in America before dialectical theology was known in Japan and before the rise of neo-orthodoxy in America. Accordingly, his own theology was formed on the foundation of liberal theology. He might, therefore, have felt isolated when he returned to Japan and began to speak his mind, since Japanese theological circles at that time were already under the overwhelming influence of dialectical theology, and especially of Barth's theology. Nevertheless, he always kept his respect for the theological heritage of the nineteenth century, as against dialectical theology, following the tradition of Schleiermacher, Harnack, and Troeltsch.

In his later years, Ariga created a stir in theological circles by insisting on hayatology in Hebrew thought as against ontology in Greek thought. According to him, *sein* cannot be conceived of apart from *werden* and *geschehen* in Hebrew thought. Although his idea was not then fully discussed in Japanese theological circles, he was ahead of his time. Nowadays, it has been discussed by E. Jüngel in his *Gottes Sein ist im Werden* (1976), and by Hans Küng in his *Menschenwerdung Gottes* (1976).

Shigehiko Sato

Shigehiko Sato (1887-1935) was five years younger than Ishihara, and older than Uoki and Ariga. Though he studied Luther, his main interests were so clearly the problems of systematic theology that it does not seem fitting to regard him only as a writer on church history or the history of doctrine. As a matter of fact, his official position was professor of historical theology at the Lutheran Seminary.

As already mentioned, Sato studied the works of Luther at the graduate school of Tokyo Imperial University, and at the same time he studied at Tokyo Theological School under Uemura. While working as a minister, he published *Young Luther* (1920), and as a result he made the acquaintance of an American Lutheran missionary, Jens Winther, who invited him to teach at Kyushu Gakuin, a Lutheran Theological School in Kumamoto. From 1922 to 1924 in Germany he studied in Tübingen and Berlin, where he devoted himself to studying Luther under Karl Holl.

As soon as he returned, Sato became professor at the Japan Lutheran Theological Seminary in Tokyo. He founded the Society for Luther Studies and published a journal, *Luther Studies,* trying to introduce Luther's ideas with great enthusiasm. Like Takakura, he died before reaching the age of fifty. However, in contrast to Takakura, who stressed the importance of Calvin and remained a dogmatician, Sato was no dogmatician and remained a scholar of Luther.

Throughout his academic work, Sato was concerned with the doctrine of faith. In other words, religious experience was his central theological concern. While in Berlin, he wrote *A Study of the Religion of Experience* (1924), stating in the preface, "The purpose of this book is to study the religion of experience, and the unique experience of religion, believing that the essence of religion is experience." In it he discussed Kant's religion of reason, Schleiermacher's religion of feeling, and Luther's religion of conscience. These discussions were to be followed by his main work, a study of Luther, based upon his doctoral thesis at Kyoto Imperial University. *Luther's Basic Thoughts on Romans* appeared in 1933, written as a result of his interest in the doctrine of faith.

Sato was critical of dialectical theology, siding with the so-called Luther Renaissance, which occupied a place somewhere between nineteenth- and twentieth-century theologies. This led to arguments with Takakura, who was sympathetic to dialectical theology.

Systematic Theology

Setsuji Otsuka

When discussing trends in systematic theology between the beginning of the Showa period and the end of World War II (1926-1945), we must, of course, mention dialectical theology, especially Barth's theology and its influence and stamp on Japanese theologians, including the five dealt with in this section. Among these Setsuji Otsuka (1887-1977) was an exception, however, because although he was stimulated by Barth, he was not influenced to the same extent as the others. This may be due to the fact that he was the oldest of the five. Although he was born two years later than Takakura and Watanabe, he was born more than ten years before the others. When dialectical theology became known, he was already over forty years old.

As soon as the young Otsuka graduated from Doshisha, he went to America, where he received a B.D. from Union Theological Seminary, and an M.A. from Columbia University. He later described his study abroad in these terms: "In America I learned from McGiffert, W. Brown and T. Hall. I attended the seminars of F. Adler and J. Dewey. I came under the influence of the Ritschlian school from the professors at Union, of the Kantian school from Adler, and of positivism from Dewey." In other words, he was deeply influenced by liberalism at that time. His master's thesis for Columbia was on Thomas Hill Green.

After his return, Otsuka taught Christian ethics and subsequently dogmatics at Doshisha. Although he absorbed something from dialectical theology, he never became a Barthian like his senior professor, Keiji Ashida. His *Prolegomena to Christian Ethics* (1935) and *Christian Anthropology* (1948) are representative of his output. The first book dealt with the place of Christian ethics in theology, the special nature and method of Christian ethics, its special features in relation to general morality, and the kingdom of God as *summum bonum*. Although it was a long book, it was intended to be an introduction to the subject; however, he never wrote the main discourse. The second book provided "descriptions of the answers by modern theologians to the basic questions of Christian anthropology," including discussions of Emil Brunner, Reinhold Niebuhr, and Otto Piper. In his later years, he published *Outline of Christianity* (1971). Though he wrote this in order to communicate the orthodox faith of Christianity, it had something of the character of an outline of dogmatics. Regarding the Atonement, he said that although he had previously regarded the punishment of God as an educational punishment, he now regarded it as retributive.

Hidenobu Kuwada

Hidenobu Kuwada (1895-1975) began his study of theology when he entered Meiji Gakuin. There was, however, no professor of systematic theology in the theological department there. It was August Reischauer, an American missionary and teacher of philosophy, who encouraged him to study systematic theology.

After graduating from Meiji Gakuin, Kuwada went on to Auburn Theological Seminary in New York, where he studied systematic theology under the young John Baillie from Scotland. Through Baillie's lectures, which were later published as *The Interpretation of Religion: An Introductory Study of Theological Principles,* Kuwada became familiar with the nineteenth-century theologians of continental Europe such as Schleiermacher, Ritschl, Herrmann, and Troeltsch. After receiving a B.D. from Auburn, he studied at Harvard Divinity School, where he majored in the philosophy of religion under E. C. Moor and was awarded an STM.

After his return, Kuwada became professor at Meiji Gakuin, and when the Japan Theological School was founded by the merger of Meiji Gakuin Divinity School and Tokyo Theological Seminary in 1930, he was appointed professor of systematic theology. Although he was then attracted by Herrmann's *Der Verkehr des Christens mit Gott,* and Otto's *Das Heilige,* he did not yet have a full theological conviction of his own. In general, his ideas were based upon Ritschlian theology. However, he turned to dialectical theology when it came to Japan. He described this experience not as a turning point but as a conversion, because through this theology he experienced a conversion of faith. He made a public confession of this conversion at a chapel service in the seminary, announcing that he had renounced liberal theology. Because Keiji Ashida of Doshisha experienced a similar turning point, the impact on liberal theology was great. When Kuwada later became president of Tokyo Union Theological Seminary he was so busy in administrative work that he could not produce any important academic work. However, he did leave his mark on the churches through his work as a theological educator. By nature a good teacher rather than a creative theologian, he trained many theological students and sent them out as ministers.

Before he became a college administrator, however, Kuwada was quite active as a writer. His representative work is *Christian Theology in Outline* (1941). The contents are an outline of dogmatics, though the title is American in style. Barth's influence is strong, and particularly noticeable in its prolegomena. He learned from Barth, he said, that theology was a science of the church and a science of revelation. One might say that this book was the first introduction to dogmatics in Japan. Although there was a book called *Dogmatics* among the collected works of Takakura, it was edited posthumously from his lecture notes. Kuwada's book was, therefore, a standard work for many years, and was compulsory reading for the ordination examination.

Kuwada also wrote *Dialectical Theology* (1933), which played a great role in introducing this theology into Japan, as well as *The Essence of Christianity* (1932) and *Understanding Theology* (1939). An article of his called "Religious Education Seen from Evangelicalism," based on a lecture given at Nikko in 1935, was memorable. Relying mainly on Brunner's *Das Gebot und die Ordnungen*, he insisted that religious education should be clearly based upon the Christian view of man. At that time there had been no discussion of religious education from a theological point of view, so this was seen as a controversial call for establishing an evangelical principle for religious education. After World War II, when John C. Bennett came to Japan, Kuwada supported his call for Christian social action. Because nobody expected this of him, it aroused a great deal of interest and comment at that time.

Enkichi Kan

The church background of Enkichi Kan (1895-1972) was Episcopalian. After studying under Seiichi Hatano at Kyoto Imperial University, he went to Harvard, where he received an STM. After his return, he became a professor at Rikkyo University, where he taught until an advanced age.

Kan learned about Troeltsch from Hatano. He wrote several articles about him and translated some of his writings. His early book *The Basic Concepts of the Philosophy of Religion* (1930) was strongly influenced by Troeltsch. At about that time, however, the Social Christian Movement developed, and both Kan and Shigeru Nakajima became active leaders in it. Another of his books, *The Turning of Christianity and Its Principles* (1930), which argues strongly for the socialization of Christianity, created a sensation. From about 1933 onwards, he began to write articles on dialectical theology for various journals. In 1934 he published *The Revival of Religion* and *The Modern Philosophy of Religion*, both of which were heavily dependent on Brunner. Thus, Kan turned from Social

Christianity to dialectical theology, responding quickly to the new trend in Europe at that time.

Since he was very responsive to new ideas, Kan was also interested in thinkers such as Paul Tillich and Nicholas Berdyaev, who were attracting attention in Europe. He introduced them to Japan and translated their works. Gradually, however, he was becoming more and more interested in Barth, among dialectical theologians. Although in 1939 he wrote a small book about Barth, called *The Theology of Barth*, he devoted himself to further study after the war, and published *A Study of Karl Barth* (1968). This was posthumously expanded and published by his widow under the title *A Study of the Theology of Barth* (1979).

Although Kan was a good translator and a reliable introducer of new theological ideas from abroad, the most representative of his own works was *Reason and Revelation* (1953), for which he was awarded a doctorate by Tokyo University. In this book, he first drew the distinction between the "philosophical" philosophy of religion, with reason as its basis, and the "theological" philosophy of religion, based on revelation. The former has reason as its basis, while the latter has revelation. Examples of the former are Troeltsch and Wobbermin; exponents of the latter are Brunner and Barth. A noteworthy feature of his work is his view of Brunner and Barth.

Brunner put forward his views on the philosophy of religion in his book *The Philosophy of Religion of Evangelical Theology*. According to him, the tasks of the philosophy of religion are to establish the relationships (1) between revelation and rational cognition, and (2) between revelation and religion. However, Barth nowhere discusses the task of the philosophy of religion. Accordingly, Kan undertakes this question himself, from the Barthian point of view. This is the unique feature of the book. According to Kan, Brunner regards revelation as the correction and completion of reason, which is distorted by sin. A presupposition of this view is that there is still a point of contact between revelation and human reason, however much it may be corrupted by sin. At the point of contact, revelation necessarily makes a connection with reason. For Barth, however, reason has no such point of contact: "The contact is made by revelation itself, or by whatever God Himself wishes." Nobody can determine how to make this contact. Understanding Barth in this way, Kan supposes the tasks of the philosophy of religion to be to answer the following questions: (1) Although theology cannot avoid using philosophical terminology, how do we deal with the problem that theology must ignore the fact that its ideas have links with the ideas contained in philosophical systems? and (2) How can the theologian indicate the limits of philosophy, which claims to be able to give ultimate answers, and how can he or she clarify the form and direction to take when engaging in philosophy?

Yoshitaka Kumano

Unlike Kuwada and Ariga, who spent their youth in an atmosphere of liberal theology, as a young man Yoshitaka Kumano (1899-1982) fell entirely under the influence of the faith and theology of Masahisa Uemura. His whole life, one might say, was to to be spent following and deepening the path laid down by his teacher in thought and theology. He received all his theological education at Tokyo Theological School, and he never traveled abroad. In spite of this, the American theologian Michalson said that Kumano's theology was "most Westernised."[3]

After graduating from Tokyo Theological School, Kumano helped Uemura, who was the editor of the journal *The New Weekly Evangelist,* and served as pastor of a church at Hakodate for several years. After returning to Tokyo, he continued his pastoral work and taught at Japan Theological School, later becoming professor at Tokyo Union Theological Seminary. He concentrated on writing rather than on ministry and education, devoting much time and effort to reading extensively in Western literature, and thus became a founder of standard dogmatics in Japan.

With Kuwada, Kumano became known for introducing dialectical theology after writing a book entitled *Introduction to Dialectical Theology* (1932). However, he was not satisfied with a mere introduction to this theology. Having absorbed its fruits, he developed his own ideas. Typical of his early works is *Eschatology and the Philosophy of History* (1933). This book stands in comparison with works on eschatology published in the West at this time. It was so widely read that the term "eschatology" became accepted in Japan. Besides publishing his private journal under the title *Protestant Studies,* he subsequently published many books, including *The Basic Questions of Christology* (1934), *A*

---

3. It differs markedly from that of Kazoh Kitamori, who was very much his junior. Kitamori did not study abroad either; and his theology has a strong Japanese flavor.

Study of the Johannine Epistles (1934), *Contemporary Theology* (1934), *The Uniqueness of Christianity* (1937), *Faith and Reality* (1941), *The Faith of the Apostle Paul* (1941), *The Problems of New Testament Theology* (1943), and *Troeltsch* (1944).

It is significant that during this period Kumano became interested in the problem of the creeds and doctrines of the church as an institution. Although this interest may have been stimulated by the contemporary discussions of church union in connection with the formation of the United Church of Christ in Japan (Kyodan), he might also have been influenced by Motokichiro Osaka, a senior disciple of Uemura. After World War II, Kumano taught Symbolics in alternate years and collected many writings on the subject. However, he published only one small book in this field, *Church and Creeds* (1942), although he was thought to be preparing a major work on this subject.

Soon after the end of the war, he published two books: *The Outline of Christianity* (1947) and *The Essence of Christianity* (1949). Although in these books, particularly in the first one, Kumano deals with the problem of the essence of Christianity raised by Harnack and Troeltsch, this does not lead him to dismiss dogmatics, as they do. Instead he uses this question as the basis of his own dogmatics. One might say that this book is the most creative of all his books. It can be read as an exposition of his doctrine of the church, showing his sympathy with Roman Catholicism and High Anglicanism. On this point, there is agreement between Kumano and Motokichiro Osaka, who was familiar with the church fathers, and who, according to Yoshimitsu Akagi, professor at Tokyo Union Theological Seminary, advocated a kind of Catholic Protestantism.

Kumano continued to be productive after the war, and published *Martin Luther* (1947), *The Synoptic Gospels* (1952), and *Introduction to Christian Ethics* (1960). Special attention should be given, however, to his *Dogmatics*, published in three volumes, in 1954, 1959, and 1965. This is his magnum opus, and represents the highest academic standard of any work to be published on the subject in Japan. After retiring from Tokyo Union Theological Seminary, he turned his attention to Japan's past and published *A History of Japanese Theological Thought* (1968). Although he began to write *A History of Japanese Ethical Thought* in the journal *Gospel and the World,* he died before he could complete it.

Kumano inherited the faith and theology of Uemura, and he never moved towards liberal theology. While Uemura's theological perspective was limited to Great Britain, Kumano's was much wider, since he had read many German theological works and had even looked into French writers on theology. Unlike Kuwada, who had turned from liberal theology to dialectical theology, Kumano had become familiar with Schleiermacher, Ritschl, and Troeltsch through their writings without becoming liberal in his own theology, and had even become interested in Dilthey. With these extensive interests, he widened and deepened his own theological position. Kumano's academic style survives in Tokyo Union Theological Seminary even to the present day. The theme of his lifework was the problem of faith and history, as it was with other twentieth-century theologians. Throughout his life he exercised all his talents in his attempts to cope with this basic problem, thereby establishing theology in Japan.

Takenosuke Miyamoto

Takenosuke Miyamoto (1905-) graduated from the department of philosophy at Tokyo Imperial University and at Takakura's invitation became a teacher at the Japan Theological School. Takakura was not only the president of the school but also Miyamoto's minister. Later Miyamoto became professor of the philosophy of religion at Tokyo Union Theological Seminary, the president of Tokyo Woman's Christian College, and the chancellor of Ferris Jogakuin.

Miyamoto was never ordained and so remained a layman. Having been strongly influenced by Karl Barth and Tokutaro Takakura, his thinking straddled philosophy and theology. Since he was also influenced by Seiichi Hatano, he inherited his philosophy of religion. He taught this subject within systematic theology at the seminary for many years. In this activity he was unique among the theological circle of Japan.

In his first book, *The Basic Problems of Christian Ethics* (1939), he considered the problems of ethics from the viewpoint of dialectical theology, making reference to Kant and Nicolai Hartmann. Since this was not merely an introduction to dialectical theology but an entirely original work based upon that theology, it made a great impression. He then published *The Philosophy of Religion* (1942), a collection of essays.

From about this time onwards, he began to consider how a Christian could engage in the study of philosophy. He published his conclusion in his book *Philosophy as Symbol* (1948). In his view, although philosophy cannot serve revelation directly in the way that theology does, it can be based on a position of love rooted in faith and can express its ideas symbolically. In other words, the Christian philosopher, being negated absolutely by the expression of the transcendent *Sache,* and subject to the limitations of his philosophical thinking, can reflect on and point out the expression of the transcendent *Sache* — in other words, he can take the path of symbolization.

Miyamoto subsequently wrote the following books: *The Logic of the Religious Life* (1949), *The Image of Man in Modern Christianity* (1958), *Seiichi Hatano* (1965), and *The Basic Problems of the Philosophy of Religion* (1968). These works show that although he was originally strongly influenced by Barthian theology, in his later years his perspective widened as he learned from Hatano and Tillich, whom he met in America. As mentioned above, Kan, who was a disciple of Hatano, discussed the philosophy of religion in his own work, but devoted himself to studying Barth in his later years without developing his own philosophy of religion. In contrast, Miyamoto was strongly influenced by Barth in his early years but remained a philosopher of religion, learning from Hatano. Miyamoto developed his own philosophy of religion.

Theologians of the Non-Church Movement

Toraji Tsukamoto

Quite a number of the disciples of Kanzo Uchimura, the leader of the Non-church group, became independent evangelists like their teacher; of these, two also became biblical scholars. One was Toraji Tsukamoto, and the other was Kokichi Kurosaki.

Toraji Tsukamoto (1885-1973) graduated from Tokyo Imperial University and worked for nine years as a government official in the Ministry of Agriculture and Commerce. Originally, he studied the Bible while working in the Ministry, but because he "could not devote himself to the work of the government in the same way as to his study of the Bible," he finally quit work and engaged in full-time biblical study. The death of his wife in the great earthquake of 1923 caused a drastic change in his life. As a result of this, he gave up his plan to study in Germany and began to engage in evangelism. In 1929 he became independent of Kanzo Uchimura and began to hold regular meetings for Bible study, which he continued until 1960, when he became ill. In 1930 he also began to publish a monthly journal called *Bible Knowledge*, which continued until 1963. Between the ages of forty-five and seventy-eight he devoted himself to these Bible study meetings and the journal.

While conducting the Bible study meetings and publishing the journal, he produced three works in the field of New Testament studies. The first was *Colloquial Translation of the New Testament*, which he completed in fourteen years between 1931 and 1944. This was a pioneer work, published by the Japan Bible Society after the war. It was included in a popular paperback series from the publisher Iwanami. The second was *A Table of the Differences in the Gospels* (1951). He completed the original manuscript of this book in three years after he began full-time study of the Bible. Though he wrote it for himself without any thought of publication, since it had survived the earthquake and his friends recommended that he do so, he finally published it nearly thirty years later. It was almost perfect in form, and of high academic standard. As he hoped, it made a great contribution to the study of the Bible in Japan. The third book was his study of the life of Jesus, which appeared in his journal *Bible Knowledge* between 1939 and 1949, as 237 lectures. Tsukamoto himself seemed to have regarded these three works as forming a trilogy. As his son-in-law Taro Yamashita said, Tsukamoto "learned and fully accepted the fruits of the biblical criticism of that time. But when he expressed his faith, he left academic studies behind and leapt into argument. Thus it was a unique life of Jesus." He was indeed an earnest student of the Bible, but above all he was a sincere believer.

According to his disciple, New Testament scholar Goro Mayeda, Tsukamoto would not have liked being called a biblical scholar, but this is what he was in the widest sense of the term. In my view he differed from the specialist particular scholar who studies the New Testament as a field of theology. Like Kurosaki, Tsukamoto followed Kanzo Uchimura and spent his life as an independent evangelist. Although he had a profound knowledge of the Bible, he never taught at a university. One wonders whether he was ever interested in so-called theology. One thing is clear, however: although he was an independent evangelist, he devoted himself to the Bible with all the academic skills granted to him. Uchimura spoke of "Tsukamoto's biblical dissipation," referring to the way he poured his all into the study of the Bible and produced so many works.

Kokichi Kurosaki

After graduating from Tokyo Imperial University, Kokichi Kurosaki (1886-1970) worked for Sumitomo, one of the largest trading companies in Japan. After the death of his wife, however, he felt called to become an independent evangelist, and spent his whole life teaching the Bible. Thus he followed the same path as Tsukamoto. Needless to say, however, he differed from Tsukamoto in his individual characteristics, following his own unique course in life.

Born the son of a Chinese classical scholar, Kurosaki became a Christian and a disciple of Uchimura in spite of his family background when he was a student at the First Higher School in Tokyo. While working for Sumitomo, he became tutor to the heir of the Sumitomo family, with whom he traveled to America. When he decided to leave the company in order to become an evangelist, many people naturally opposed his plans. The reasons for his father's objections are interesting. The first was that he had not fully repaid the favors received from the Sumitomo family. The second was that if one teaches "the way," one should teach it only to those who seek it rather than sell it on the street. Since his father was loyal to his feudal lord, who was opposed to Western culture, Kurosaki's conversion to Christianity might have meant his abandonment of his traditional spiritual environment. However, in old age Kurosaki commented that although he had become an independent evangelist against his father's will, he had actually spent his life in the same way as his father. Just as his father spent his life teaching the Chinese classics, so he spent his life teaching Christian scriptures.

A year after resigning from Sumitomo, Kurosaki went to Europe to study. At first he studied in Berlin; then he moved to Tübingen, where he met Karl Heim, who recommended that he publish his conversion experience under the title *Bekehrung eines Gottlosen*. He then went to Geneva and studied Calvin with E. Choisy, returning to Japan via Great Britain and Palestine.

After his return, Kurosaki began in 1926 to publish a monthly journal, *The Eternal Life;* and from 1930 on, he began to hold meetings for Bible study in the Kansai area, including Osaka, Kyoto, and Kobe. He also engaged in writing a number of books. His journal was banned for some time because he criticized the Japanese government's policies after the Manchurian incident, and because he bitterly criticized Hitler. It was not until after the war that this journal resumed publication, and it continued until 1966.

Like Tsukamoto, Kurosaki also concentrated on studying the Bible. However, since he studied theology under Heim, his interests were much wider than Tsukamoto's. On the other hand, while Tsukamoto's works were more specialized, Kurosaki's were more popular. His first work consisted of his Bible studies, which appeared in his journal for forty years. The second was the series of *New Testament Commentaries* that was started in 1929 and was completed in 1950. The third was the *Old Testament Short Commentaries* in three volumes, written jointly with a number of friends. The fourth was *New Testament Concordance,* whose Greek-Japanese part was published before the war, with the Japanese-Greek part being completed after the war.

As these works show, Kurosaki studied the Bible with unfailing patience and steadfast energy. Like his friend Tsukamoto, he also lived his life for Bible study. However, as already shown, he was also interested in theology. Besides a book on Calvin, he wrote several articles on the doctrine of the church. He tried to think through the Mu-kyokai (Non-church) theologically and also discussed the question of sanctification.

Catholic Theologians

Although today the Catholic Church produces quite a number of theologians, during the period between 1912 and 1945 there were not very many. Here we will mention only two: Soichi Iwashita and Yoshihiko Yoshimitsu.

Soichi Iwashita

Soichi Iwashita (1889-1949) was born into a wealthy family and was baptized during his junior high school days. After graduating from

Tokyo Imperial University, where he studied philosophy, he taught at the Seventh Higher School in Kagoshima. In 1918 he was awarded a scholarship from the Ministry of Education to study in Europe. After studying at the Catholic University of Louvain in Belgium, St. Edmund's Seminary in England, and the Propaganda Seminary in Rome, he was ordained priest by the archbishop of Venice in 1925. Returning from abroad, he began to spread Catholic thought through his energetic program of study and writing. Even though he became the head of a leprosy hospital, he continued to study and write until his death. His contributions to missionary work and intellectual work are remarkable. He is remembered as the scholar who laid the foundations of the study of European medieval thought in Japan. As a Catholic theologian he gave leadership to the Japanese Catholic Church through his many writings.

In his student days, Iwashita was influenced by von Koeber. In his early years he had a great respect also for von Hügel, and later for Garrigou-Lagrange. His academic interests were not only in the church fathers and scholastic philosophy, but also in modern thought, especially that of Martin Luther. He wanted to study Luther from a Catholic point of view because he believed that Luther had distorted European thought. He hoped in this way to demonstrate the orthodoxy of the Catholic tradition.

As his disciple Yoshihiko Yoshimitsu said of Iwashita, he was not the type of scholar who constructs a system by reflecting on metaphysical ideas, but he was convinced that he could demonstrate, both theoretically and practically, the most vital truth of Christ in terms of the historical reality of the religious life. For instance, although his friends wanted him to return to academic life, he dedicated himself to the work of the leprosy hospital, which made a deep impression on the public. This decision apparently arose out of his piety and participation in the sacrifice of Christ.

Typical of his work was the posthumously published *The Deposit of Faith* (1941), which consisted of theological essays that had appeared in the journal *Catholic Studies* and which discussed the question of the authority of the Catholic Church, the priesthood and sacraments, justification and sanctification, and similar matters. *The Study of the History of Medieval Philosophy* was also published posthumously. It contained other works of his which had been published previously, such as *Medi-*

eval Currents of Thought (1928), *Neo-scholastic Philosophy* (1932), and *Augustine's "City of God"* (1935).

Yoshihiko Yoshimitsu

While Yoshihiko Yoshimitsu (1904-1945) was a student at Tokyo Imperial University, he came under the influence of Iwashita and was converted to Catholicism. After graduating, he went to France and studied neo-Thomism with Jacques Maritain. In 1933 he returned and taught at Sophia University and the Catholic Seminary. He married, but his wife died within three months. He then became a leader of the Catholic student movement. In 1935 he was appointed a lecturer in ethics at Tokyo Imperial University, and he engaged in writing with great energy. He died of lung cancer in 1945.

Side by side with Iwashita, Yoshimitsu was an intellectual leader of Catholics in Japan, although he died before being ordained priest. Most of his writings were not purely theological, but dealt with the philosophy of religion and Christian philosophy, with particular reference to *Geistesgeschichte*. Since there was no tradition of studying European medieval thought at Tokyo Imperial University, his attention was drawn first to this field of study by Iwashita through the reading of Aquinas's *Summa Theologica*, second to neo-Thomism by Maritain in Paris, and finally to modern Catholic thought through correspondence with Erich Przywara of Munich.

During the ten years between his return to Japan and his untimely death, Yoshimitsu wrote many articles that showed that his contribution was more than simply introducing neo-Thomism. He also paid attention to modern thought, which he regarded as a disease, insisting that the cure for it was Thomism. Yoshimitsu was very much interested in those thinkers who had described the crisis and tragedy of modern thought and who tried to find a way out of it, such as Pascal, Kierkegaard, Nietzsche, and John Henry Newman. When discussing these thinkers, he sympathized with the agony of modern man and expressed his personal view that there is salvation in agony.

Yoshimitsu was also deeply interested in literature and often discussed Dostoevsky, Rilke, and Péguy; in fact, he came to be called a poetic philosopher.

He wrote the following books: *Catholicism, Thomas, Newman* (1934),

The Basic Problems of Cultural Ethics (1936), *Poetry and Love and Existence* (1940), and *The God of the Philosopher* (1947). After his death, Yoshimitsu's collected works were published in four volumes: Volume 1, *The Idea of Culture and Religion* (1947); Volume 2, *A Study of Medieval Geistesgeschichte* (1948); Volume 3, *A Study of the History of Modern Philosophy* (1949); and Volume 4, *Mysticism and the Modern Age* (1952).

From the Prewar to the Postwar Periods

The decade leading up to the end of the war, 1935-1945, was a period in which Barthian theology had such an overwhelming influence that it almost became the orthodoxy of Japanese Christianity. During this period, Barth reached volume 2/1 of his *Church Dogmatics* and was far removed from the scholasticism of what is known as Barthian dogmatics. That the spirit of Barthian theology, whose characteristics are expressed in the theology of the word of God, the theology of revelation, and concentration on Christology, had a dominant influence on Japanese Protestant theology at this time is undeniable.

Postwar theology must be understood in the light of this prewar situation. Nobody rivaled Kano Yamamoto in his firm attachment to Barthian orthodoxy. In 1947 he published *Politics and Religion — How Did Barth Fight?* which introduced the Barth of the *Kirchenkampf.* Later he wrote a major work, *Theology of Heilsgeschichte* (1972), under the overwhelming influence of Barth.

However, some theologians tried to overthrow this Barthian orthodoxy. Kazoh Kitamori (1916-), in his *Theology of the Pain of God* (1946), which laid stress on the God of love who suffers pain, criticized Barth's theology with its emphasis on God in contrast to man and on the first commandment as a theological axiom. He saw this as a theology that laid stress on the God of law. Naturally, Barthians reacted strongly against Kitamori.

Jiro Ishii (1910-87) wrote *A Study of Schleiermacher* (1948), the result of solid research. Its purpose was not to promote Schleiermacher as a rival to Barth. Rather it was an apologia of Schleiermacher in response to Barth's and Brunner's criticisms. According to Ishii, Schleiermacher's theology is not a form of subjectivism, as Brunner alleged, but a *höehere Realismus,* as Hatano saw.

Kazuo Muto (1913-1995) is another theologian who has tried to take a different course from Barth. Like Enkichi Kan, he also stands for a "theological" philosophy of religion as against a "philosophical" philosophy of religion. His goal is to make the philosophy of religion a medium between theology and philosophy. According to Muto, the earlier philosophical philosophy of religion sought to make reason the medium between theology and philosophy, so that theology lost its autonomy. On the other hand, Barth's and Brunner's theology, by their insistence on the self-contained completeness of theology, deprived philosophy of its autonomy. In contrast to these two positions, Muto found in Kierkegaard's religious existentialism a model of a theological philosophy of religion which does not deprive theology and philosophy of their own autonomies but which mediates between them. His book *Between Theology and Philosophy* (1961) articulates this perspective.

The tendency to oppose Barthian orthodoxy can be seen more clearly among the younger generation, who began to study theology immediately after the war. Toshio Sato (1923-), though paying respect to Barth, studies nineteenth-century theology, as Barth did, but in his case in order to confront Barthian theology. In his *Modern Theology* (1964), he deals with Schleiermacher, Ritschl, Herrmann, and Troeltsch. Subsequently, his published work has taken two directions: one in the field of dogmatics, learning from Barth; the other in the field of cultural ethics, learning from Troeltsch.

Yasuo Furuya (1926-), who had learned about Barth from Kano Yamamoto and who was encouraged by Yoshitaka Kumano, wrote a dissertation at Princeton on the absoluteness of Christianity. In this, too, one sees an awareness of the questions at issue between Troeltsch and Barth. Although Furuya has produced many studies of American Christianity, he has maintained an interest in the question of the relationship between Christianity and other religions, and published a work entitled *Theology of Religions* (1985).

Hideo Ohki (1928-), who had learned from Brunner in Japan and was stimulated by Troeltsch's ideas, wrote a thesis on Puritanism under Reinhold Niebuhr at Union Theological Seminary. He was the first to introduce covenant theology and Puritanism's idea of natural right to Japanese Christianity. As his first book *Brunner* (1962) showed, he originally valued Brunner more highly than Barth. But gradually he became more interested in Barth and wrote a study of him, entitled *Barth* (1984).

Yoshinobu Kumazawa (1929-) also learned from Brunner in Japan, and was interested in Bultmann. He wrote a thesis on hermeneutics in Heidelberg. His first book, *Bultmann* (1962), became a standard and was a pioneering work in the field of hermeneutics, an area in which interest was first aroused after the war.

Although there are other theologians to be considered, they will be dealt with in the next chapter. Here we have limited ourselves to consideration of certain aspects of the postwar theological atmosphere that succeeded the Barthian orthodoxy of the war period.

CHAPTER 3

The Third Generation, 1945-1970

SEIICHI YAGI

A General View

THE UNCONDITIONAL SURRENDER of Japan in 1945 had certain consequences for the country because the war in the Pacific was characterized by four aspects:

1. Imperialism: After achieving partial modernization by adopting the capitalist system, Japan began to colonize neighboring countries and invaded China.
2. Nationalism: The war led to resistance on the part of traditional Japan to the country's domination by Western civilization. The liberation of Asian countries from Western colonialism was one of the stated main aims of the war, but the truth was that Japan wanted to replace the Western world powers.
3. Government by the emperor, which was linked to Shintoism.
4. Totalitarianism: The war was conducted in a totalitarian state of emergency under the emperor, who was regarded as divine.

These four aspects of the war produced four corresponding consequences after the surrender:

1. The breakdown of the old system and increasing interest in or sympathy for communism; the "anti-status quo movement" in general, especially among intellectuals.

2. Almost complete lack of respect for Japanese tradition, and admiration of Western culture, including Christianity.
3. The separation of church and state in the new Constitution.
4. The democratization of Japan — possibly the most important consequence for the development of Japan in the postwar period.

Under her new constitution, Japan renounced imperialism and the right to declare war, thereby expressing her will to remain a minor power. However, the increase in tension between the USA and the USSR encouraged the growth of the capitalist system in Japan, and the country moved towards becoming a world economic power. These features of Japan's economic and political situation immediately after the war were reflected in the philosophical life of the country. An interest in communism, Christianity, and existentialism played an important role. Interest in the latter originated in the overthrow of nationalism, which led people to query the meaning of human existence.

Though Christianity had not been prohibited by the state during the war, it was regarded as Western and thus harmful to the nation. Quite a number of Christians supported the war in order to demonstrate their loyalty to Japan. However, after the war the situation changed, and Christianity began to attract many people. The numbers of Christians and the influence of Christianity on intellectuals grew rapidly. The Christian church, however, was very different from what it had been before the war. It was much more socially oriented, and it attacked social injustice. There were even Christian communists. On the other hand, Christianity had to provide answers to the existential questions, and this led to the development of existential Christian theology. These circumstances led the West-oriented church to seek a standpoint which would guarantee not only its independence, but also the purity of Christian faith in a non-Christian milieu. This is why Karl Barth's theology was welcomed so enthusiastically. Christians criticized the Emperor system and the union of the state and religion, which was seen in the Yasukuni cult (the deification of the war dead). They were also critical of the "imperialist" growth of the Japanese economy.

The surrender also brought about a radical change in the country's value system, prompting many young people to realize the lack of justification for the status quo. The shock of the breakdown of those values that young people had previously believed to represent the highest good led them to a radical questioning of the basis of all authority. Among some young Christians, this led to a critical inquiry into Christianity and its foundations. This included a readiness to encounter other religions, especially Buddhism. On the other hand, the effort to learn Western theology continued unchanged into the postwar period.

This short survey, which is necessarily simplified, provides a tentative introduction to the circumstances of the immediate postwar period. Let us now turn to some more concrete examples.

For some years after the war, Karl Barth's theology was studied with great enthusiasm. He had already had a considerable influence in the 1930s, but now his theology became dominant in Protestant churches in Japan from the end of the war until the end of the 1960s. Emil Brunner's stay in Japan in the 1950s, his teaching, and his efforts to build a bridge between the church and the Non-church Movement were remembered by the Japanese church for a long time. Though he was highly regarded in Japan, his theology did not become the dominant tendency because of the Japanese Protestants' intense interest at this time in Barthian theology, which rejected Brunner's *theologia naturalis*. Typical of the theologians who remained faithful Barthians after the 1970s was Kano Yamamoto, who wrote *The Theology of Heilsgeschichte* in 1972.

The young theologians who had studied in the United States introduced the ideas of Reinhold Niebuhr and Paul Tillich and translated their major works into Japanese. From the end of the 1950s onward, Rudolf Bultmann and his school found support in important circles. The tension between Bultmann and Barth was reflected in theological discussions in Japan on the problems of historical criticism, hermeneutics, the historical Jesus, etc. At this time the study of the Bible became largely independent of the church and become the subject of university scholarship.

It is also worth noting that interest in Dietrich Bonhoeffer was growing during this period. In the second half of the 1960s attention was also paid to J. Moltmann and W. Pannenberg, whose major works were being translated into Japanese, accompanied by comparative studies of their theologies. Naturally, American theology also aroused interest. To give one example, H. Cox's *The Secular City* was translated; and the death of God theology was discussed. Advances were made in the study of the history of theology, as well as in systematic theology and in biblical scholarship.

The following are important works in systematic theology and the history of theology from this period: Yoshinobu Kumazawa, *Bultmann* (1962); Toshio Sato, *Modern Theology* (1964) and *Loss and Restoration of Religion: Secularization as the Destiny of Christianity* (1978); Hideo Ohki, *Ethical Thoughts of Puritanism* (1966); Yuzaburo Morita, *The Modernity of Christianity* (1973); and Keiji Ogawa, *Subjectivity and Transcendence* (1975).

The authors named above, as well as other theologians who taught in departments or schools of theology, played leading roles as representatives of the church scholarship of this period, which was overwhelmingly dominated by the West. However, in this situation they wanted to move forward, and they made a substantial contribution to raising the level of theological studies in Japan. Nevertheless, we will not discuss the content of their work in this chapter. Instead, we will present the work of those thinkers who, working more or less in isolation, remained of necessity theological outsiders, teaching for the most part in secular colleges, although their works were often very widely read.

Characteristic of this period was the foundation of major societies for the study of theology: Japan Society of Old Testament Studies (1933, refounded in 1947); Society for the Study of the History of Christianity (1949); The Japanese Biblical Institute (1950); Japan Society of New Testament Studies (1960); Zen-Christian Colloquium (1967); and Japan Society for Buddhist-Christian Studies (1982).

Between 1969 and 1972 almost all the universities in Japan were shaken by violent student movements, and the Christian universities were no exception. As a result, the courses in Christianity in the literature department of Aoyama Gakuin University, Tokyo, and in the department of theology of Kanto Gakuin University, Yokohama, were cancelled.

Having concluded this general survey, we will now proceed to the discussion of individual theologians and their work.

Kazoh Kitamori and the Theology of the Pain of God

As a young theologian, Kazoh Kitamori, at that time an associate professor at Japan Theological Seminary (now Tokyo Union Theological Seminary), published *The Theology of the Pain of God* in 1946 — one year after the Japanese surrender — causing a sensation among the Christian readership of Japan. The mere fact that a Japanese had written an original work of systematic theology, thereby becoming the first original theologian in Japan, was a surprise in itself. Kitamori, who was born in 1916 and graduated from the Lutheran School of Theology in 1938 and from the philosophy department of Kyoto Imperial University in 1941, had written a theological essay on the pain of God during his school days (1936). The idea of the pain of God came to him through his own efforts to understand the gospel correctly and appropriately, and at that time he already saw the pain of God as the core of the gospel.

According to Kitamori, the pain of God means that God loves the object of his wrath, namely sinners, while his love overcomes his wrath. This also means that the God who loves and the God who feels wrath are one and the same God. God loves those whom God cannot love naturally. He gave the world his only Son. In the sense that God's love overcomes God's wrath, God is entirely the God who embraces. However, God's love is by no means an immediate love, but a love that is mediated by and based upon pain. God is not simply the God of wrath, nor the God of simple love. Thus Kitamori saw the very essence of the gospel in the pain of God.

Does this mean that Kitamori holds a patripassianist view of God? Answering this question, Kitamori made a distinction in the book between God the Father, who suffers pain, and God the Son, who died. It is God the Son who suffered on the cross, not God the Father. The Father suffers pain because of the death of the Son. He insists that the theology of the pain of God is therefore by no means heterodox. Insisting on the correctness of his interpretation of the gospel, he goes on to criticize Karl Barth. For Barth, God is not really the God who embraces, because his dominant idea is the exclusiveness of revelation, the opposition between God and the world, and the qualitative difference between them. On the other hand, Kitamori criticized liberal theology because it preaches a God whose love is an immediacy without pain. He also criticized Hellenistic Christianity, which speaks of God in ontological categories, thus losing sight of the God who suffers pain. According to Kitamori, German theology did not sufficiently restore the idea of the pain of God.

For Kitamori, human pain is an analogy, a symbol, of the pain of God. Of course, human pain is qualitatively different from divine pain, because the former is the result of human sin, which is the object of divine wrath. However, both pains have something in common, so that the former can serve as an analogy for the latter. Kitamori finds one instance of this analogy in the concept of *tsurasa,* characteristic of Japanese literature. Tsurasa consists of the suffering of the one who, in order to save the others whom he loves, inflicts pain upon himself or upon his son, even going so far as to put him to death. In other words, the cultural tradition of Japan can be meaningful as a preparation for understanding the gospel. (The fact that tsurasa is an analogy for the pain of God might have given consolation to those who experienced tsurasa during the war.)

A Christian can become one with God as in mysticism, according to Kitamori, but it is impossible to become one with God in one's own immediacy. However, it is not true that oneness is simply impossible. God and a human being immediately become one in pain, that is, in that which denies immediacy. Pain is, on the one hand, the negation of the immediate oneness of a human being with God. Nevertheless, there is within pain a mystic oneness of humanity and divinity. Such mysticism does not reject ethics, but rather posits it. God's self-denial is a basis for human self-denial, as well as a request for it. Divine pain thus becomes human pain, which leads to the ethics of loving one's enemy.

On the basis of the pain of God, Christian eschatology is seen in the following way: the end of history comes when the gospel is preached all over the world (Matt. 24:14). The consummation of the pain of God is the necessary condition for the advent of the end of history. Thus the Son of Man suffers first, and the end of history cannot come until the pain of the world reaches its consummation.

The Theology of the Pain of God became so well known that Kitamori was regarded as *the* theologian of Japan. However, his theology was not highly regarded by specialist theologians. In the first place, his ideas were held to be patripassianist, in spite of his denial. Second, he criticized Barthian theology at a time when it was predominant. A third reason may perhaps be that Kitamori held a positive attitude towards the cultural tradition of Japan at a time when Japanese tradition as a whole was regarded very unfavorably. Kitamori should have presented the history of the conception of the pain of God more fully in order to show that it was not heterodox. He met with more acceptance among Mu-kyokai Christians and philosophers. In the 1960s, the suffering of God became a popular subject in European theology. There, Kitamori's theology was reviewed by such theologians as D. Sölle, J. Moltmann, and H. Küng. *The Theology of the Pain of God* was translated into several European languages, and today it seems to be attracting more attention in Japan.

Sakae Akaiwa and the Exodus from Christianity

Sakae Akaiwa was not an academic theologian but a pastor. What chiefly interests us is the course of his life, rather than his writings. Akaiwa was born in 1903 in the Ehime Prefecture of Shikoku, graduated from the Tokyo Theological Seminary (now the Tokyo Union Theological Seminary) in 1928, and was ordained in 1932 as a pastor in the Japan Church of Christ (now the United Church of Christ in Japan). Thereafter he successfully devoted himself to mission as a Protestant pastor and to writing. In the 1930s he came under the influence of Karl Barth and was regarded as one of the most enthusiastic Barthians.

After the Japanese surrender, Akaiwa became increasingly sympathetic to Marxism. He did not accept Marxism out of any conviction of the historical necessity of the transition from capitalism to Marxism. Instead, he understood the human being not only as a creature facing God but also as a person in an I-Thou relationship and as a member of society. He understood humanity in its totality and called this understanding "humanism." Thus behind his sympathy with Marxism lay his humanism based on the experience of what his encounter with Jesus had taught him about human nature.

Akaiwa could not agree to the use of violence to advance the Marxist revolution. However, he held the capitalist system to be no less violent, and he finally declared his intention of joining the communist party in 1949, although at that time it was quite unusual for a Christian to become a Marxist. He did not, however, put this decision into practice, presumably either because the communist party hesitated to accept him or because he took care not to upset his church too much. Theologically speaking, he could not support Marxism as a whole. He was afraid of the perversion of the truth in Marxism's absolutization of the politico-economic aspect of human life, which suggests that in the last resort human beings exist for the sake of Marxism.

Akaiwa began to move away from Barthian theology after about 1955. This move took place, as he himself described, in the following way. Akaiwa read Barth's book on Mozart, in which Barth said that he did not know whether Bach was played in heaven, but that he was sure that when the angels were together on their own they played Mozart and that God enjoyed listening to them. Akaiwa wondered how Barth, a mere man, knew so much about God. This led to his antipathy towards Barth as a man, and later developed into antipathy towards Barthian theology as a whole. In March 1959 he sold all his volumes of Barth's *Church Dogmatics,* his former pride and joy, to a secondhand bookseller. With the proceeds, he invited his friends to a restaurant in Tokyo and celebrated his liberation from Barthian theology with good champagne.

According to Akaiwa, Barth had been his superego. Under its heteronomous control, he had striven to propagate Barthian theology, but finally he became aware of what he was doing. Akaiwa's acquaintance with German New Testament criticism also contributed to his liberation. It convinced him of the rightness of historical, critical studies of the Bible.

In 1964 Akaiwa wrote *Exodus from Christianity,* in which he described his exodus not only from Barthian theology but also from Christianity. To summarize, this book maintains that the Gospels are not historical records of Jesus, and that the categories and conceptions of Pauline theology are mythological. This book is not an original work. In it he merely confirmed in his own way the commonly held views of critical New Testament scholarship of the postwar period. However, Akaiwa reached these conclusions quite honestly, believing there is no foundation for traditional Christianity. Accordingly, he rejected the Bultmannian form of interpretation, which, while accepting the preaching of the apostles, tries to remove existential self-understanding from the New Testament. He discarded Christianity, including apostolic preaching. Thereafter he showed deep sympathy for Buddhism, especially Zen Buddhism, seeing ultimate reality in *sunyata* (emptiness). S. Yagi, who became acquainted with Akaiwa late in life, may have influenced his thought. However, Akaiwa died of cancer of the liver in 1966 before expounding the significance of Buddhism for Christianity.

Exodus from Christianity aroused a great deal of reaction, mainly hostile. Rinzo Shiina, one of the best-known novelists at that time, was a member of Akaiwa's church. He was baptized by Akaiwa in 1950 and was a regular contributor to *Yubi,* a Christian journal that Akaiwa edited. However, as Akaiwa became more critical of traditional Christianity, tension grew between the two men. Finally, in 1964 when Akaiwa published *Exodus,* Shiina stopped contributing to *Yubi* and began to attack Akaiwa in print. In 1966, Shiina even published a novel, *Good Demon,* in which he caricatured his former teacher. The United Church of Christ in Japan was naturally opposed to Akaiwa's views as well. Many theologians, including Kitamori, thought that Akaiwa had overstepped the bounds of Christianity. Some even thought that he should be dismissed from membership in the church; however, his death prevented this from being carried out.

In his later years, Akaiwa denied what he had earlier actively promoted, and he died before fully developing his new position. He was in a state of constant movement and transition, as if he represented in himself the whole history of theology in Japan in the twentieth century. Thus there is no single Akaiwan theology. One thing remained unchanged throughout the whole of his life, however: his relationship with Jesus. In his school days, he wrote that he encountered God through Jesus. As stated above, Akaiwa was a self-declared humanist, and his humanism was based on his encounter with Jesus. In his Barthian period, he said that he did not know God, but that through his relationship to Jesus he felt his relatedness to the reality that Jesus called Father. In his later years, he wrote that Jesus called forth the ultimate subjectivity within him. Because he was familiar with New Testament criticism, he knew that his encounter with the Gospels was not *ipso facto* his encounter with the historical Jesus. Jesus was for him, so to speak, the symbol of *sunyata,* because his encounter with the Jesus of the synoptic Gospels revealed to him what *sunyata* was. What he found after all was the fact that the encounter with Jesus of the Gospels revealed to him the ultimate, upon which he based his humanism. He called this God or *sunyata,* depending upon the particular situation.

Nobuo Odagiri and his "Christology"

Nobuo Odagiri was neither a professor of theology, nor a pastor, but a layman, a medical practitioner by profession, who wrote simple Christian literature. We refer to him in this context because the naïve questions he raised about traditional Christology aroused intense interest in the subject within Japanese Christendom. Born in Hokkaido in 1909, he graduated from the medical school of Hokkaido Imperial University in 1934, but did not practice medicine until after the Second World War. He had attended the kindergarten attached to the Sapporo Independent Christian Church, was baptized in 1927, and became an active member of the church. In 1949, while participating in the reconstruction of the Sapporo City YMCA, he had a problem with one article in its program. It declared that the YMCA had faith in Jesus Christ, as God and Savior, based on the testimony of the Bible. However, to Odagiri the Bible did not say that Jesus Christ was God. In fact, he was not "biblicistically" interested in the Bible. For him the core of the Christian message was the atoning death of Jesus Christ on the cross for our sins, and the Christian faith was above all the faithful acceptance of this message. He thought that since God could not die, Jesus' death on the cross could have been nothing more than a drama, not a real death, if Jesus had been God. Such a view would destroy the gospel.

After making a thorough study of the biblical testimonies, Odagiri began to insist that Jesus Christ was not God, but the Son of God. This insistence was surely "biblicist," because he asserted that there was not a single sentence in the Bible which unambiguously identified Jesus with God, nor could he find evidence of a trinitarian view, according to which Jesus was the second person of the Trinity, God the Son. His view was based on his faith in the soteriological significance of the death of Jesus on the cross, which would lose any meaning if Jesus were immortal God. It was the Son of God who became incarnate, died, and rose again. He argued that the Bible was consistent in this respect.

At first, Odagiri's Christology was merely a matter of concern for the YMCA. However, he wanted to open up the problem to the Christian public at large so that it might be discussed at an academic level. Thus he came to Tokyo in 1952, and working there as a medical practitioner, he tried to organize a project team for the discussion of Christology. In 1955 he conducted an open debate with Kitamori and others in a Christian journal *Kaitakusha*. Since Kitamori's "pain of God" presumes the unity of the trinitarian God as well as the distinctions, he was critical of Odagiri's views. Furthermore, Kitamori affirmed the existence of biblical testimonies to the divinity of Jesus Christ. Odagiri did not submit to Kitamori's criticism, but counterattacked and continued to put forward his own views. In 1960 he visited Germany at the invitation of the North German Mission to give lectures and to conduct discussions with theologians at Hamburg University.

Besides setting up the project team for discussing Christology, after his return to Japan in 1957 he sponsored a series of lectures on Christology by more than twenty distinguished theologians. These lectures were published in 1968 as *Christological Studies*. Among the contributors are most of the theologians who are discussed in this book.[1]

A Debate on Buddhism and Christianity

Katsumi Takizawa and Seiichi Yagi will receive fuller treatment in the next chapter; nevertheless, since they took part in the dialogue between Buddhism and Christianity in the 1960s, which led to a twenty-year-long debate between them, they deserve mention in this chapter. Takizawa, who published *A Study of Karl Barth* in 1941, had already attracted the attention of theologians before the Second World War, but became prominent as a philosophical theologian after the war.

Takizawa was born in the Tochigi Prefecture in 1906 and entered the law school of Tokyo Imperial University in 1927. However, the only effect the lectures had on him was to make him question the basis of law and justice. Because the lectures failed to satisfy him, he transferred to Kyushu Imperial University in 1928 — an unusual procedure at that time — to study philosophy. In spite of studying European philosophy intensively, he found no solution to the doubts concerning the meaning of human life that had gripped him in his boyhood. He finally experienced enlightenment, something like "the scales falling from my eyes," while struggling with the works of Kitaro Nishida (1870-1945), a Zen philosopher and founder of the so-called Kyoto school of philosophy.

---

1. Odagiri ought to have entered into dialogue with Katsumi Takizawa, who will be discussed in the following section. If this had happened, a new perspective would have been opened to Odagiri on the relationship between the Logos, Jesus, and Christ. I often urged him to give serious consideration to Takizawa's views. However, Odagiri and Takaziwa, who contributed to *Christological Studies,* showed no interest in each other's work.

Takizawa suddenly understood what Nishida meant by his formulation of "the Identity of the Absolute Contradiction."

In 1933 he published an article, "General Conception and the Individual," in the philosophy journal *Riso*. This was an attempt to interpret Nishida, who on reading the article wrote a letter of congratulation to Takizawa. From then onward, he remained on intimate terms with Nishida, although he had not studied under him at Kyushu Imperial University. In 1934 before Takizawa went to Germany on a Humboldt scholarship, he asked Nishida with whom he should study. Nishida encouraged him to go to Karl Barth because "he spoke of God better than M. Heidegger." As a result, Takizawa went to Bonn to study with Barth and became one of his favorite students.

After his return to Japan, Takizawa taught the philosophy of religion in the department of philosophy at Kyushu University from 1947 to 1971. In 1965 and 1974, and again from 1977 to 1978, he was in Germany as a visiting professor. In 1984 the department of theology of Heidelberg University awarded him an honorary degree for his contributions to dialogue between Buddhism and Christianity, as well as between theology and philosophy. However, immediately before his planned departure for Heidelberg, he died of leukemia.

In 1964 Takizawa published *Buddhism and Christianity*, a critical essay on the philosophy of religion of Shin-ichi Hisamatsu (1889-1980). A student of Nishida, Hisamatsu was at that time emeritus professor at Kyoto University and was a great Zen master as well as a Zen philosopher. As a Zen Buddhist, he maintained an "atheism," but not, it should be noted, atheism for which human beings and the world exist, but God does not exist. Hisamatsu rejected theism. According to him, God or Buddha, as objective beings, are an illusion. There is no Buddha apart from the one who is awakened to the Formless Self (the ultimate object both in and of the person), which is realized in the person as the true Self when the old ego has died in confrontation with the absolute contradiction of being and non-being, value and non-valuelessness. The true Buddha is the "Buddha who I am." The objectified Buddha or God is at best a secondary construction.

In his *Buddhism and Christianity*, Takizawa acknowledged the genuineness of Hisamatsu's religion, never treating it as a pagan fallacy. On the other hand, however, Takizawa criticized Hisamatsu, pointing out that he made no clear distinction between the Buddha as the ultimate and the Buddha who everybody could become. To go into further detail, in this book Takizawa drew a distinction between the primary and secondary contacts of God with the human being. The primary contact is the primordial fact of Immanuel (God with us), or in other words, Christ. This is the fact which lies at the basis of every person, quite unconditionally and regardless of what that person may or may not have done, and whether the person is a Christian or not. However, not everybody is aware of this fact. When one has been awakened to the primordial fact, one becomes aware of its activity, and a religious life is realized within oneself. Takizawa called this event the "secondary contact of God with the human being." According to him, both Buddhism and Christianity are genuine religions, based on the primordial fact of Immanuel, and each represents the secondary contact; thus Buddhism is a sister religion to Christianity. Buddhists, however, do not make this distinction between the primary and secondary contacts of God with the human being. While insisting upon the inseparability of the primordial fact and the form it takes in the secondary contact, they elevate enlightenment to the position of the measure of all religious matters.

Takizawa also criticized traditional Christianity in the following terms. Christianity, though generally making the strictest distinction between the two contacts, does not distinguish them in the person of Jesus. According to him, Jesus was a man who realized the secondary contacts so fully that he became the model for all human beings. This does not mean that the primary contact was established by Jesus. Nevertheless, traditional Christianity, including Takizawa's teacher Karl Barth, has held that the primary contact came into existence through Jesus Christ. (We must add that Jesus has been held to be the primary contact itself.) Thus Jesus was made the Savior, and Christianity has laid claim to exclusive absoluteness. For Takizawa, the primary contact itself must be clearly distinguished from Jesus as one form of the secondary contact, however normative he may be. Takizawa, having expounded his views in this and many other books, gained a wide readership among Christians as well as Buddhists, but only limited approval among professional theologians, most of whom had nothing to say on his views.

Thereafter he described the relationship between God and human beings in the primary contact as "inseparable, unidentifiable and irreversible"; he also described the relation between the primary and secondary contacts in the same way. The fact that "irreversibility" was regarded as problematic by those who had accepted Takizawa's distinction led to controversy. Ryomin Akizuki and Masao Abe, both Zen philosophers, and Masaaki Honda and Seiichi Yagi, Catholic and Protestant theologians respectively, joined in, and the resulting discussion was published as *Buddhism and Christianity: Seeking a Dialogue with Takizawa* (1981), edited by Yagi and Abe. As a Buddhist, Abe insisted on the basic reversibility of all relations. Akizuki stood for a functional irreversibility; Yagi saw a moment of irreversibility in the relation between the Self and ego, while divinity and humanity formed a unity in the Self. Showing considerable insight into the issue, Honda proposed the following formulation: reversibility and irreversibility condition each other.

The aspect of irreversibility was discussed because the relation between the basing and the based is, generally speaking, reversible in Buddhism (Abe's thesis), whereas the relation between God and human beings is irreversible in Christianity. Takizawa followed Nishida in "inseparability and unidentifiability," and followed Barth with his "irreversibility." Probably Takizawa should examine the ontological quality of the primary contact. Though the existence of the primary contact itself cannot be denied, it is not unconditionally actual as it is. Just as Christ had been virtually unreal to Paul (who had been determined from before birth to be the Apostle to the Gentiles) until the Son of God was revealed to him (cf. Gal 1:15f.), the primordial fact is virtually nonexistent for those who have not been awakened to it. It does not work in and to them, so that they respond to it with awareness. In Zen, too, the Buddha nature, which is inborn in everyone, is nevertheless virtually unreal unless one is awakened to it. There is a paradox here in that the primordial fact becomes actual simultaneously with the event of the secondary contact. The primary contact is therefore actualized for the first time in the secondary contact, in and to the awakened. In this sense we can say that the primary contact was fully established (actualized) for the first time — at least in Christian eyes — in and as Jesus. Naturally, this does not mean that the exclusive actuality of the primary fact is limited to Jesus alone. Its actualization is possible at any time and in any person. Gautama Buddha, for example, attained it. The primary fact is actual in and as the awakened one, and nowhere apart from "Buddha who I am," as Hisamatsu said. Hisamatsu is right in this respect. On the other hand, Paul, for example, was aware of the distinction as well as of the unity of his ego with Christ (cf. Gal 2:20). In the relationship between Paul and Christ there is a moment of irreversibility. Takizawa is right in this respect.

It is regrettable that Hisamatsu did not answer Takizawa, for both of them have now died. However, the matter that concerned them must be thoroughly investigated because the distinction that Takizawa drew is of considerable significance for Christology. While recent New Testament scholarship has made a diachronic distinction between the Jesus of history and the Christ of kerygma, Takizawa drew attention to a synchronic distinction between Jesus and Christ, so that Christianity becomes in principle intelligible to everyone. This distinction is naturally significant for the dialogue between Christianity and Buddhism because it shows not only the possibility of, but also the necessity for, real dialogue, not mere comparisons, between Buddhists and Christians. In this way, Takizawa opened the way to overcoming the Christian claim to exclusive absoluteness, which is everywhere regarded as problematic. This achievement is of extreme importance for Japanese Christians in their encounter with Buddhism. They are still too easily inclined to sympathize only with the Pure-Land-Buddhists' faith in Amida Buddha, while holding Amida Buddha to be an idol (a tendency among Protestants); or to learn from Zen Buddhism only methods of meditation, without a real understanding of Zen (a tendency among Catholics).

A theologian who has posed significant challenge to Takizawa's thought is Seiichi Yagi, born in 1932 in Yokohama. His father had been a student of Kanzo Uchimura. While a student at Tokyo University, Yagi became a Christian through reading the works of Kierkegaard and Uchimura. He did postgraduate work on the New Testament under Goro Mayeda in the same university. Among his fellow students were Akira Satake, Sasagu Arai, and Kenzo Tagawa, who will be mentioned in the following sections. From 1957 to 1959 Yagi studied theology at the University of Göttingen. Attending Ernst Käsemann's lectures on St. Matthew's Gospel there, he learned to accept the methods of historical criticism in full. He then devoted himself to reading the works of Rudolf Bultmann and became heavily involved in "demythologizing."

It was at this time, while in Germany, that he encountered Zen Buddhism for the first time. During his stay there he was often asked about the teaching of Buddhism; however, as a Christian, he had taken no specific interest in this religion and had only an elementary knowledge of it. Ashamed of his ignorance, Yagi read some of the books on Buddhism that another student had brought with him, among them books on Zen by D. T. Suzuki. But to Yagi's astonishment he could not understand them at all. This experience caused him an existential crisis. In 1958 he visited Wilhelm Gundert, who had come to Japan at the beginning of this century and got to know Uchimura and his pupils, including Yagi's father. After Gundert's return to Germany, he taught Japanese studies at Hamburg University. When Yagi visited him, he was emeritus professor and was living in Ulm, a beautiful city in South Germany. He was engaged in translating *Bi-yen-lu,* a classical work of Chinese Zen, into German. Yagi knew little of this, for he visited Gundert simply because his father sent him to see an old friend. As Yagi took his leave of Gundert, the latter accompanied him to the station, and gave him an offprint of his translation of the first chapter of *Bi-yen-lu,* together with the Chinese original and a detailed commentary. On the journey back to Göttingen, Yagi read this over and over again until, totally exhausted, he paused absentmindedly, and understanding suddenly flashed upon him.

Yagi soon became aware of the parallels between his first religious experience, when he became a Christian, and his second one in the train; and this parallelism shed a new light on his first experience as liberation from the determining power of language. Before he became a Christian, morals had been the primary determinant of his behavior. What he had seen as a personal encounter was in reality merely an encounter between his ego and moral codes, or to put it another way, his superego had been the ultimate subject of his person. However, he had not been aware of that. As he became a Christian, he sympathized with Paul's saying that Christ lived in him (Gal 2:19f.), and he naturally understood this realization as salvation, because of Jesus Christ's atonement. Now his second experience showed him clearly that what he had regarded as an encounter with objective beings was in reality merely the encounter between his ego and the bearers of the names, or else he had read the idea into the beings which he "encountered" and held it to be their reality. Something like an invisible wall had concealed reality as it was. The subject-object distinction and the conceptions of the beings — namely, the inevitable construction of our language — had pretended to be the primary reality as it was.

Through this parallelism, Yagi came to know the reality of "immediate experience" prior to the invisible wall, in both the phases of subject-object (Buddhism) and I-Thou (Christianity) encounter. As he gradually came to understand, the realization of the immediate experience prior to language construction opens up a way to the actualization of religious life, because our use of language gives rise to the ego, leading to egocentricity. Thus immediate experience is a way of overcoming the absolutization of the ego and realization of the Self, the ultimate subject of a person. The more Yagi considered this matter, the more convinced he became that Zen had at least a parallel "existential self-understanding" with Christianity. This was the term he used at that time, for he was engaged in interpreting the self-understanding of the New Testament. This made him aware of the relativity of Christianity, and led him to see the basis of Christianity not in the death, resurrection, and atonement of Jesus Christ, but in the Logos, which worked everywhere to actualize religious experience.

After his return to Japan, the department of theology of Kanto Gakuin University employed him as a full-time lecturer in New Testament studies in 1960. However, he left the department in 1965 because of the tension caused by his critical view of traditional Christianity and transferred to the Tokyo Institute of Technology, where he stayed until 1988 as professor of German.

In 1963 Yagi published *The Formation of New Testament Thought*, in which he made the following points, although his thoughts were not yet fully developed. The Christ-kerygma of primitive Christianity — including that of Jesus' resurrection — is to be understood as the interpretation of the enlightenment event in a fashion peculiar to that time. The event itself is parallel to Zen Buddhism. Therefore we do not need to presume direct intervention by a supernatural power in order to understand the formation of the New Testament kerygma. In the enlightenment event, the absolutization of the ego is overcome. This consisted largely of the fallacy of holding the secondary construction of our language to be primary. In fact, on the contrary, reality means the mutual penetration of subject and object, I and Thou, Self (Christ living in me) and ego. He called the event in which the invisible wall vanishes and the mutual penetration becomes intuitively visible "pure intuition," avoiding the term "pure experience" used by Nishida because this did not seem correct to him. According to Yagi, the New Testament as a whole can be understood through "pure intuition." In this book his chief thesis was that the language of the New Testament could be understood without making any critical judgment on its truth. The publication of the book was a significant event for Japanese Christendom.

Takizawa, a well-known authority, read Yagi's book and wrote *The Biblical Jesus and Modern Thinking* (1965) as a response to the work of this young, unknown beginner in theology. Although he regarded Yagi's book highly in some respects, he criticized it on three points:

1. Yagi explains the formation of the ideas of the New Testament without critically examining their veracity.
2. Like Bultmann, Yagi does not understand the transcendent.
3. Yagi's "pure intuition," like Nishida's "pure experience," does not provide any satisfactory basis for religious cognition.

For his part, Yagi had read Takizawa's *Buddhism and Christianity,* and had immediately agreed with the distinction he drew between the primary and secondary contacts of God with human beings. In 1965 Yagi read Takizawa's criticism of his book and acknowledged the justice of his criticism on the first and second points. Yagi did not yet have an adequate word for the True Self at that time. However, he could not agree with the third point of criticism, regarding it as a lack of understanding on Takizawa's part. Whatever name is given to the "pure intuition" ("immediate experience" may be a better term), Yagi maintained, it is an event in which one becomes aware that our uncritical use of language creates something like invisible walls. Yagi wrote a defense of Takizawa's criticism, *The Biblical Christ and Existence* (1967), in which he agreed with Takizawa's distinction between the two contacts, and, admitting the validity of his criticism on the first and second points, tried to show that his own position was not essentially different from Takizawa's. However, this did not satisfy Takizawa, and although he accepted Yagi's works for a doctoral thesis, he continued to attack him on the third point. This was the beginning of a debate between these two in which Akizuki later participated.[2] Yagi did not change his views, and the debate continued both in public and in private until Takizawa's unexpected death in 1984.

2. See Takizawa, Yagi, and Akizuki, *Where God Is to Be Found* (1977).

From the beginning, Yagi was under the impression that Takizawa, who had a clear understanding of the Self (the actuality of the primary contact), had not had the immediate experience in the phase of the subject-object encounter; and furthermore, that he did not argue on the basis of experience, but on the basis of Nishida's ambiguous description of the experience. The more he debated with Takizawa, the more convinced of this he became. Meanwhile Yagi carried on dialogues with Shin-ichi Hisamatsu (*The Religion of Awakening* [1980]), and with Keiji Nishitani (1900-1990), a Zen philosopher. This dialogue was published in 1989 under the title *Immediate Experience*. Throughout these dialogues, Yagi remained convinced of the invalidity of Takizawa's criticism on the third point. As Takizawa did not retract his views either, the debate between them did not lead to any consensus. However, the debate did cause Yagi to submit his views to philosophical consideration and to develop his standpoint in order to meet Takizawa's criticism. In this way, Yagi became involved in the philosophy of religion, moving away from the field of New Testament studies through dialogue with Buddhism, all the time trying to throw light on the essence of Christianity and Buddhism through interreligious dialogue. Since 1988 he has been teaching philosophy and ethics at the Toin University of Yokohama.

Yoshio Noro and Existential Theology

Yoshio Noro deserves to be mentioned here because he published his first major work, *Existential Theology*, in 1964. Noro was born in Tokyo in 1925. After graduating from the Japan Theological Seminary, he went to the United States and studied at Drew Theological Seminary and Union Theological Seminary, where he obtained the degree of Th.D. in 1955. From 1956 to 1972 he taught systematic theology in the literature department of Aoyama Gakuin University, Tokyo. In 1970 he took the degree of Litt.D. at Kyoto University. When he was dean of the department of literature at Aoyama Gakuin University, the students' movement led to his transfer to the course on Christianity in the literature department of Rikkyo University, Tokyo, where he remained until 1992 as professor of systematic theology.

Existential Theology was written in opposition to the current theological climate in Japan, which was largely determined by the controversy between the followers of Karl Barth and Rudolf Bultmann. At that time the traditional Japanese church was afraid that Bultmann's existential methodology might destroy Christian faith, the church, and theology. On the other hand, some young theologians were introducing up-to-date German theology into Japan. In this period, which may to some extent be regarded as critical, Noro published this book in order to show that existential theology could in fact strengthen the church and theology; however, it expressed more sympathy for Paul Tillich than for Rudolf Bultmann.

In *Existential Theology* Noro criticizes Barth on the one hand for his system of theology "from above" which makes dialogue with the modern world impossible. On the other hand, however, Noro rejects radical demythologization because the Christian faith needs myths. In his view, human existence gains authenticity when it responds to God, who was revealed in Jesus Christ, and who speaks to human beings through the salvation event of Jesus Christ. He calls this "human destiny." In other words, revelation provides the answer to the existential question of human beings. In this respect, Noro is close to Tillich's apologetic theology. However, the basic theme of his book is the I-Thou relationship, in other words, personal encounters of the sort described by Martin Buber. Indeed, Noro is critical of Tillich's theology because it is too ontological to remain faithful to the personality of God and human beings. In the same way, he also criticizes Takizawa's philosophical theology.

Noro, who was a good friend of Odagiri, admits the latter's influence on his own interest in Christology. But the essence of Noro's own Christology can be seen in his statement that the historical event of Jesus Christ, as it happened, is the action of God. In so saying, Noro draws a distinction between the dimension of historical facts and that of historical significance. He takes the distinction further into "dimensional thinking," according to which reality has many opposite, un-unifiable dimensions, so that we have to go deeper into one dimension in order to open the way to the others. The relationship between history and theology, natural facts and God's action, are to be understood in this way. This reveals his sympathy with F. Gogarten. In short, his conception of human existence consists of its personality, which is realized when the human being responds to the call of God.

With this as his starting point, Noro understands history not as being determined by God, but as a drama of dialogue played out between God and human beings, neither of which can foresee the course of history. He upholds human life after death because each human being is loved by the eternal God as a partner in God's dialogue, so that the human being cannot be brought to naught. Furthermore, human beings can live a full life in this world under the premise of life after death, and it is precisely this circumstance which postulates our life after death. In this argument, Noro reminds one of Kant.

In light of this discussion, one may ask whether there is a preceding human postulate for a full life, which is then realized by revelation; or whether revelation negates human religious wishes once and for all, in order for divine grace to bring it to realization. In his book *Between Theology and the Philosophy of Religion* (1961), Kazuo Moto argued in favor of the second alternative, looking for the paradoxical unity of faith based on revelation and human religious experience. Against this view, Noro seems to incline to the first alternative, and this tendency becomes increasingly clear in his later years.

Noro's later works include *Existential Theology and Ethics* (1970), *John Wesley: His Life and Theology* (1975), and *God and Hope* (1986). In this latter work he sets out his theology almost in the style of a book review, discussing numerous European and American theological works, especially those of process theology, but completely ignoring Japanese theologians, except for Kitamori and Odagaki, both of whom he treats critically. It is difficult to summarize the contents of this book. However, the fundamental motifs are clear. While examining suffering, the irrational, *nihil,* death and so on, that is, those matters which lead humans to despair, Noro nevertheless states the grounds for hope. On the basis of his *Existential Theology,* he begins to discuss the world and history as the *topos* of human existence. Since God is a person and not the ground of being, God is an entity, not the absolutely absolute, but the relatively absolute. Referring to J. Berdjajew and J. Böhme, he says that God is eternally born from *nihil,* creates out of *nihil,* and in fighting against it, overcomes it. According to Noro, *nihil* is common both to God and human beings, but there is no evil in God, since evil could never be removed from this world if it originated in God. He approaches the irrational in the same way.

Human life is too incomplete and brief for human existence to attain unity with God, so Noro introduces the idea of *samsara*. After innumerable rebirths into this world, human existence achieves its fullness. The introduction of *samsara* into theology seemed odd to many Christians. However, since Noro affirms life after death while denying the existence of the other world to which the dead go, he must admit *samsara*. According to Noro, *samsara* does not mean permanent suffering. If "pain" were an attribute of God, as Kitamori insists, suffering could not be removed from the world of humanity. Therefore neither pain nor suffering belongs to God. We need God, who loves us, because we are too weak to bear absolute solitude. Therefore God exists, and we are immortal. We have no guarantee of the consummation of history, which is reached when history ends and the kingdom of God comes about. We can still hope to enjoy the moments when justice and love are exalted, or, to put it another way, we can hope to experience the fullness of human existence.

Noro affirms his belief in *samsara,* which Buddhism has overcome both theoretically and practically. However, he does not approve of dialogue with Buddhism because he sees in interfaith dialogue merely an effort to concentrate on the features common to Christianity and Buddhism, while overlooking the individuality and essence of each.

New Testament Scholarship in the 1960s:
Kenzo Tagawa and Sasagu Arai

Because modern New Testament scholarship mainly deals with very specialized problems, it is difficult to write a general history of it. In the following passage we will only consider studies of interest to a wide readership. More specialized studies and their authors are not mentioned, not because they are insignificant, but because it would be impossible to deal with them adequately. We will simply list some of these works here without discussing their contents. Notable works published between the 1950s and 1970s include Goro Mayeda, *Introduction to the New Testament* (1956); Hideyasu Nakagawa, *Studies on the Letter to the Hebrews* (1957); Jisaburo Matsuki, *The Letter to the Romans* (1966), *New Testament Theology I* (1972), and *The Relation of Jesus to the New Testament* (1980); Akira Satake, *The Letter to the Philippians* (1969), *The Letter to the Galatians* (1974), and *The Apostle Paul* (1981);

and Shin-ichi Matsunaga, *Body and Ethics: The Theology of St. Paul.* (1976), among others.

Academic study of the Old and New Testaments had begun, as indicated in the previous chapter, before the Second World War. After the war, in the 1960s, biblical studies were undertaken in the universities, thus becoming largely independent of the church. This was mainly the work of Masao Sekine and Goro Mayeda, two Non-church scholars. Both studied in Germany and taught at state universities, Sekine teaching the Old Testament at Tokyo Pedagogical University, and Mayeda the New Testament at Tokyo University. Japanese state universities have no departments of theology because of the separation of church and state in the constitution. They have courses on the academic study of religions, but no institutes for clerical training. Akira Satake, Kenzo Tagawa, Sasagu Arai, and Seiichi Yagi, the New Testament scholars mentioned in this book, all studied the New Testament with Mayeda before continuing their studies in Europe.

Kenzo Tagawa was born in 1935 in Tokyo. In 1958 he graduated from Tokyo University, and after doing postgraduate studies in the New Testament there he went to Strasbourg to study with E. Trocmé and published *Miracles et Évangile* (1966). After his return, he wrote *A Phase of the History of Primitive Christianity* in 1968. In this book, which I consider to be one of the best studies of St. Mark's Gospel, he applies the methods of redaction criticism, which Hans Conzelmann had developed in *The Centre of Time*, originally entitled *Die Mitte der Zeit* (1953) to the study of Lucan theology.

According to Tagawa, chapters 14-16 of St. Mark's Gospel are a later addition. In this, he is following his teacher Trocmé. More interesting is his view of the Evangelist's understanding of Jesus. He argues that Mark is Galilee oriented, meaning that Mark not only collected oral traditions about Jesus in Galilee himself, but that he deliberately wrote his Gospel in opposition to the Jerusalem-based Christ-kerygma, which preached Christ as the Son of God, the eschatological figure who died and was resurrected, and who would soon appear from heaven. As in the case of St. Paul, this says almost nothing about Jesus of Nazareth. Mark, however, saw the *Evangelium* — good tidings — in the fact of Jesus' appearance on earth.

This Jesus of Nazareth was something extraordinary, astonishing, and fearful — something that could not be named by traditional titles such as the Son of God, Lord, Savior, etc., as in the Christology of the Jerusalem school. Mark's Jesus forbids his disciples even to talk about him (Mark 8:30). Unlike the Jesus of Matthew, Mark's Jesus does not accept Peter's confession: "You are the Christ." Jesus' disciples, as depicted by Mark, are completely incapable of understanding him. In this, Mark insists that the error of Jerusalem Christology lies in its view that Jesus can be comprehended by giving him christological titles. Accordingly, any attempts by scholars to reveal Mark's theology, as if, like Matthew and Luke, he had wanted to elucidate the significance of Jesus by the use of theological concepts, misses the point. Rejecting this methodology, he remains a simple narrator of Jesus' life without using christological concepts at all.

Although younger than Akaiwa, Tagawa was a good friend of his, and after Akaiwa's death he succeeded him as editor of *Yubi*. Tagawa, who had been a full-time lecturer in New Testament studies at the International Christian University in Tokyo, was dismissed because at the time of the students' movement he attacked the university administration, supporting the students and refusing to give lectures. He then taught at the theological seminary in Zaire. After returning to Japan he has taught religion since 1978 at the Osaka Prefecture Women's University. Meanwhile, he has written an excellent commentary on Mark (vol. 1, 1972), and a work on Jesus, *A Man Called Jesus* (1980). In this work Jesus is described as a man who, standing on the side of the people suffering under the double oppression of the Romans and the ruling Jewish stratum, dared to offer a "paradoxical opposition" to the rulers. Thus, for example, the words of Jesus in Luke 6:29 — "When a man hits you on the cheek, offer him the other cheek too; when a man takes your coat, let him have your shirt as well" — are to be understood as the expression of desperate rage: "When a man of power comes and hits you on the cheek, present the other cheek to him. It cannot be helped. When a usurer comes and strips you of your coat, throw your shirt at him, too, saying, 'You are welcome to it!'" All of Jesus' words and deeds are presented in this way.

Sasagu Arai, the son of a pastor, was born in 1930 in the Akita Prefecture. In 1954 he graduated from Tokyo University, then did postgraduate studies there in Primitive Christianity. In Germany he studied under E. Stauffer in Erlangen, obtaining a Th.D. in 1962. After returning home, he taught Primitive Christianity in the literature department of

Aoyama Gakuin University. In 1969, during the students' movement, he transferred to Tokyo University, staying there until he retired in 1991. Arai published the following studies on gnostic religion: *Christologie des Evangeliums Veritatis: eine religions-geschichtliche Untersuchung* (his doctoral thesis, 1964) and *Primitive Christianity and Gnosticism* (1971), which won a Japan Academy prize. He then turned to the study of the New Testament, writing *Jesus and His Time* (1974); *Commentary on the Acts of the Apostles* (vol. 1, 1977); and *Jesus Christ* (Studies on the Synoptic Tradition and Synoptic Gospels, 1979).

Almost simultaneously with but independent of G. Teißen, Arai developed the method of literary sociology. His *Jesus and His Time* is a product of this approach. His method consists of drawing inferences from the bearers of the Jesus tradition. While form criticism, particularly as represented by D. Dibelius, found the origin (*Sitz*) of the Jesus tradition in the actions of the earliest Christians, Arai drew attention to the importance of the social strata to which they belonged. Those who handed down the miracle stories belonged to the lowest stratum of society. Characteristic of this tradition is the "order to go home" (e.g., Mark 1:44; 2:11; 5:10). This command of Jesus to people of the lowest stratum in society, who were not admitted into family and ordinary society, answered their desire to enter the home. In this injunction Jesus is disturbing the social order.

Analyzing the tradition of Jesus' own words, Arai infers that the bearers of this tradition belonged to the petite bourgeoisie in its use of words such as *property, speculation, bank, credit, employment, banquet,* etc. In contrast to the miracle stories, this tradition contains Jesus' orders to leave family and society. Arai infers from this that the ethos of the petite bourgeoisie at that time included attachment to the religious community. In any case, Jesus' words unsettled the everyday social order by responding to the needs of the people. In this way Jesus was in conflict with the ruling stratum of society, which benefited from a stable social order. Jesus' criticism of the law and temple cult amounted to criticism of the status quo of that time. By so doing, he stood side by side with the disadvantaged, who were called sinners, and devoted himself to ensuring that they might live a full human life in a community free from discrimination.

One of the problems associated with Arai's *Jesus and His Time* is that any correspondence between the Jesus traditions and social strata is at best a matter of statistical probability, not of exclusive necessity. It is unlikely that there was no one among the petite bourgeoisie who related the miracle stories. Nevertheless, Arai argues as though all those associated with the miracle stories belonged to the lowest classes, and that accordingly they had knowledge of Jesus' orders to leave family and society. Furthermore, how did Jesus' faithful observance of the law (e.g., Mark 1:44) shake the social order? Arai sees in Jesus' observance of the law a sense of realism; however, it seems that this does not provide an adequate solution to the problem. These issues did not prevent *Jesus and His Time* from gaining a wide readership not only among Christians but also among non-Christians, particularly in the "anti–status quo" current of opinion then to be found in Japan.

Old Testament Studies after the Second World War: Masao Sekine

There was remarkable progress in Old Testament studies after the Second World War. The 1950s were the time for learning from Europe and the United States. From the 1960s onward, specialists in the Old Testament who had studied in Europe or the United States began to publish monographs of a high standard. Before discussing Masao Sekine in particular, we should mention a selection of other important works: Koki Nakazawa, *Studies on Deutero-Isaiah* (1963); Kiyoshi Sakon, *Studies on the Psalms* (1972); Ken-ichi Kida, *Israelite Prophets: Their Duty and Writings* (1976); Koichi Namiki, *Ancient Israel and Its Surroundings* (1979); Toshiaki Nishimura, *Prophecy and Wisdom in the Old Testament* (1981); and Yoshihide Suzuki, *Philological Studies on Deuteronomy* (1987). Since the 1970s, works of Japanese scholars such as Tomoo Ishida, Fujiko Kohata, and Akio Tsukimoto have been published in the monograph series *Zeitschrift für die Alttestamentalische Werke*, an international journal for Old Testament studies. One of the characteristics of Old Testament studies in Japan is the adoption immediately after the war of the sociological method of Max Weber, whose *Das antike Judentum* was translated by Yoshiaki Uchida in the years 1962 to 1964. An example of this trend is the work of Koichi Namiki, who has recently been applying Weber's methodology of comparative sociology to his study of the Old Testament.

Masao Sekine has had a far-reaching influence on Japanese Christendom, not only as an Old Testament scholar, but also as a theologian. Born in Tokyo in 1912, he graduated in 1935 from the law school and in 1944 from the literature department of Tokyo Imperial University. In 1944 he obtained a Th.D. from Halle University, and in 1962 a Litt.D. from Tokyo Pedagogical University, where he taught between 1954 and 1976. In 1971 he received an honorary degree from the theological department of the University of Erlangen, in Germany.

Sekine is one of the leaders of the Mu-kyokai (Non-church). As a student he became closely acquainted with Julius Schniewind in Germany, and this had a profound effect upon him as a Christian. As a Mu-kyokai theologian, he holds firmly to the standpoint of the theology of the cross. On the other hand, some of the key concepts in his Old Testament interpretations, such as "paradox and analogy," were taken from Shishio Nakamura (1889-1968), a Protestant philosopher of religion. A further influence on Sekine's approach to the philosophy of religion was the Kyoto school of philosophy.

Sekine's works cover a wide range of Old Testament studies: (1) his own translation into Japanese of the Old Testament, which is widely read by non-Christians as well as by Christians; (2) commentaries on books of the Old Testament, such as *The Book of Jeremiah* (1964), *The Book of Job* (1970), and *The Psalms* (1972); (3) monographs, such as *The History of the Religion and Culture of Israel* (1952), *The Old Testament: Its History, Literature and Thought* (1955), *The Thought and Language of Israel* (1962), a collection of essays, *A History of Old Testament Literature*, 2 vols. (1978-80), and *Thinkers of Ancient Israel* (1982); (4) numerous essays on the Old Testament in European languages as well as Japanese; and (5) essays, monographs, and lectures on Mu-kyokai and the Christian faith.

Sekine trained many Old Testament specialists, thus raising the study of the Old Testament in Japan to an international level. Characteristic of his work is his logical formulation of the thought of the Old Testament, employing the concepts of the Kyoto school of philosophy on the basis of his linguistic, philological and historical investigations. He does not present the thought of the Old Testament systematically in the form of an Old Testament theology. Rather, following the stream of Old Testament thought diachronically, he describes its content at each stage of its history synchronically — a method appropriate to its nature. Thus, for example, he understands Old Testament prophecy as follows: a prophet (the individual) removes the people's illusion (the particular) as if they were naturally united to God (the general) in order to announce anew the unity grounded in the grace of God. His view of the role of the prophets, formulated in logical terms, has much to do with his insight into the Christian faith. In both cases, human unity with God in natural immediacy is rejected, to be restored on the basis of soteriological mediation.

Examining Sekine as a theologian, we must remember that he is a Mu-kyokai Christian. He was a member of the group led by T. Tsukamoto, and in his youth he came to faith in Jesus Christ because of his death of atonement on the cross. After the war Sekine participated for a while in the ecstatic speech movement begun by a charismatic leader who appeared among Mu-kyokai Christians. However, he soon realized that this spiritual faith lacked the "word of the Cross," and so left the movement. Since that time the relationship between spirit and word has been a grave problem for him. Indeed, it is also a difficult problem in Old Testament interpretation. On the one hand, the spirit is at work through the mediation of the word; but, on the other hand, spiritual experiences exist in their immediacy. Leaving the ecstatic speech movement, Sekine found that there was a state of "faithlessness of the religious." In this state he again encountered Jesus, who had been forsaken by God in the name of God. His standpoint of "faithlessness as faith" was that of a person crying, "I have faith. Help my faithlessness" (Mark 9:24). Faithlessness in this sense is not the rejection of faith, which is a decision which shuts out every possibility of faith. It is rather something beyond the opposition between the human decision to believe or not to believe. One is reminded of the *Mu* (nothingness) of Mu-kyokai, which, while in no way rejecting the church, declares that the invisible church is beyond human organizations. A Buddhist might call *Mu* in this sense *sunyata* (emptiness), and a Christian might interpret this *Mu* as the absolute Yes and No which God says to everything that is human. This excludes any positive meaning ascribed to human deeds merely on the basis of humanity. Similarly, Sekine speaks of "lovelessness as love" and "hopelessness as hope." One may regard this as Sekine's interpretation of the Protestant principle of "by faith alone," which is, according to Sekine, intensive spirituality.

This spirituality seems to be an immediate religious reality of divine origin which is not grounded in the word of apostolic preaching; one would like to see in this a point of contact with Nishida's philosophy. On the other hand, Sekine has firmly maintained his faith in Jesus' atonement on the cross, on which his preaching is centered. He therefore objects to demythologizing as well as to a pluralistic theology of religion. In spite of his sympathy with the Kyoto school of philosophy, he remains critical of dialogue with Buddhism. One would like to ask him what the relation is in his view between spiritual immediacy and faith as the acceptance of the word of the gospel. He does not seem to make the relationship altogether clear, although both moments are tentatively united in his sacramental understanding of the wholeness of personality. In this sense he is faced with the problem of the relation between the Christian faith (word) and Buddhist enlightenment (immediacy), and one might expect him to attempt to resolve this question.

Conclusion

Japanese theology in the period from 1945 to 1970 was predominantly christological. It provided a foundation for the following period in which theological reflection on God was to be demanded. Thus the history of Japanese theology enters into a new phase.

CHAPTER 4

Theology after 1970

MASAYA ODAGAKI

The Post-1970 *Zeitgeist*

DIVIDING POSTWAR THEOLOGY into two periods, pre- and post-1970, has not always won public acceptance. Therefore I want, first of all, to make clear the meaning of this division, and at the same time to establish the methodological standpoint of this chapter.

I have called the period before 1970 the "classic age" of contemporary theology. In this period theological giants such as Barth, Bultmann, and Tillich were playing active roles, and dialogue with these great theologians was the basic method of doing theology in this country. In fact, some have called this the period of the "Germanic Captivity." In particular, the theology of Karl Barth, who emphasized the qualitative difference between God and man, was so influential that many theologians felt it necessary to enter into theological and ethical dialogue, whether in agreement or disagreement, with him. However, this theological mood changed significantly after 1970. A certain theological journal in Japan has described this change as creating the "post-Barthian age." Though this expression has no more theological justification than the "post-Bultmannian age," it expresses this change in the theological state of affairs in this country.

A distinctive feature of the way of thinking after 1970 is the exodus from the subject-object concept. The theologian who opposed this exodus most vigorously was, needless to say, Barth, together with Bultmann and Tillich, who objected to the scientific thinking of modern theology. However, in opposing modern theology, they necessarily pre-supposed its existence as the object of their objections. Thus they had not wholly freed themselves from the thinking that they opposed — they needed modern theology as the negative postulate of their own theology. To use Karl Popper's terminology, their relation to modern theology was "falsificationism."

The exodus from subject-object as the characteristic way of thinking after 1970 meant getting rid of even the falsification relationship towards modern subject-object thinking. Attention must be drawn to two matters at this point.

First, the knowledge that was sought after 1970 was to be founded on *meontology*, that is to say, the ontology of nothing. (*Me* in Greek means conditional negation, as distinct from *ou* which means absolute negation; hence, meontology is ontology of nothing in the Heideg-gerian sense.) Knowledge cannot be grounded in the object in the subject-object schemata. This is the very problem of contemporary epistemology, or theory of knowledge, and must therefore influence contemporary theology. We can no longer consider God as an entity confirmable in the subject-object framework.

The understanding that God does not exist as a reality is already to be found in Barth and Tillich, although they do not seem to be keenly aware of the meaning of this. It may be said that the task of theology after 1970 is to clarify what this means, since this has remained unclear in their thought. Can we not say that meontological epistemology, that is to say, the understanding that knowledge and interpretation are founded on what is unidentifiable as an entity, is the post-1970 *Zeitgeist* — to use a favorite word of the Germans — which is not restricted to the world of theology? For example, the problems of language since the time of Heidegger (Jacques Derrida and Richard Rorty's insistence upon deconstruction; Thomas Kuhn's reconsideration of the legitimacy of scientific knowledge) are all fundamentally related to this meontological thinking. Michael Polanyi's "tacit knowing" and Whitehead's "process philosophy" are also connected with meontology, though Polanyi and Whitehead belonged to earlier generations. The problem is this meonto-logical reality, and I want to call this reality "the post-1970 *Zeitgeist*."

The second point is that this meontological post-1970 *Zeitgeist* has a kinship with the Oriental thought of *Mu* (Nothing). It is a well-known fact that Allen Ginsberg and Gary Snyder, leaders of American counterculture, were interested in Oriental thought. Heidegger felt a great sympathy with Daisetsu Suzuki's book on Zen. Seisaku Yamamoto writes that Whitehead has something in common with Kitaro Nishida (*Whitehead and the Philosophy of Nishida,* 1985), and Robert Magliola has pointed out the similarity between Jacques Derrida's thought and Oriental thinking (*Derrida on the Mend,* 1984). Going beyond the contradiction and confrontation between subject and object means seeking for something that is neither objective nor subjective. It is therefore understandable that such a something cannot be grasped by the subject, and will become Nothing within the framework of modern scientific epistemology. This comes close to the Oriental idea of Nothing. By using the expression "post-1970 theology," I mean a theology developed within this kind of *Zeitgeist.*

Post-1970 theology has been strongly influenced by the philosophy of Kitaro Nishida (1870-1945). Before Nishida, the principal occupation of philosophy had been commenting on and elucidating imported Western philosophy. It has been said that Nishida created an original Japanese philosophy by adopting and at the same time criticizing Western philosophy, which was based on being, approaching it from the Oriental standpoint of Zen Buddhism, the characteristic of which was Nothing. The Self-identity of the Absolute Contradiction, the central concept of Nishida's philosophy (though strictly speaking, it is not a concept), is very reminiscent of the *coincidentia oppositorum* of Nicholas of Cusa. Nishida expressed the place or field where the opposite poles in the contradiction were accepted in one vision as the Absolute Nothing, while Nicholas of Cusa regarded it as the holy darkness. The fact that theology since 1970 has been influenced by Nishida's philosophy means, therefore, that we have now begun to establish an original Japanese theology which has adopted the Oriental ideas of Nothing and Field.

The point at issue is the change in the theological climate described above. The year 1970 is not always such a clear dividing line as was 1919, the year of publication of Barth's *The Epistle to the Romans,* which marked the beginning of contemporary theology. However, a distinct change in ways of thinking took place around 1970. We can indicate two reasons for this. The first is the rebellion of young people that occurred all over the world at about this time. The counterculture movement, which prevailed from the late sixties to the early seventies, was young people's desperate protest against contemporary technocratic society, in which people were dehumanized and controlled in such a way that even their protests had been controlled by society. In their despair at such a situation, young people tried to live by a qualitatively different value system from that of modern Puritan morality. This movement was not a falsification protest against the modern spirit, but an attempt to live in an entirely different spirit, which refused to accept modern consciousness even as the object of their protest. This movement represents the same *Zeitgeist* as that of the university conflicts that began in 1968 with the May Revolution in France and spread all over the world from that time onward. The students realized that no protest within a value system can be effective in resolving a contradiction within that system. The prevailing consciousness itself, they believed, needs to be transformed. I want to include this awareness as part of the post-1970 *Zeitgeist*.

Second, the university conflicts had a great influence on Christian universities and theological schools as well as on the church in Japan. Young Christians protested against the sophisticated and authoritative nature of established Christianity in Japan. However, the university and church authorities could not provide an effective response to the rebellious young people. Unable to understand that what they were calling for was a changed awareness, not merely a simple alteration to the system, the authorities reacted oppressively. Two departments of theology (Aoyama Gakuin and Kanto Gakuin Universities) were closed down during the disturbances. Although there may be different views about the conflicts themselves, the conflicts in the church around 1970 urged us to reconsider what kind of theology should be developed in this country. In any case, since 1970, theology has been built upon a rather unstable foundation.

The task of the present chapter is to look back over the theological situation in the very near past while maintaining the standpoint stated above. However, I do not mean to imply that theology as it has developed since 1970 has been formed in such a way as to satisfy the needs of the present time. Rather, it is a theology which insists that the God of Christianity is primarily and originally meontological, and that God as *totaliter aliter* cannot be other than meontological. If we can say that theology *before* 1970 is christologically oriented, then theology *after* 1970 is a theology centered on the doctrine of God. The theology to be discussed below will be explained from the viewpoint of how meontological intentions are carried out by each theologian.

The Influence of Meontological Thought

Katsumi Takizawa

The theology of Katsumi Takizawa (1909-1984), the late professor emeritus of Kyushu University, had, in my opinion, the underlying intention of taking a step further the meontological element of theology that had remained undeveloped in Karl Barth. This is our reason for dealing with Takizawa in this chapter. As we have seen above (pp. 93-97), Takizawa was the first theologian to draw a comparison between Christianity and Buddhism, not on the level of the study of comparative religion, but on the level of the "being" of religion.

In Takizawa's book *Buddhism and Christianity* (1964), he followed Barth in saying that humanity's fundamental way of being is Emmanuel (God with us). Emmanuel is the *Urfaktum* that exists unconditionally of itself, preceding any man-made distinction between God and man, faith and unfaith, Christian and non-Christian, etc. We say that Emmanuel has something in common with Nishida's Self-identity of the Absolute Contradiction (between God and man). God, who confronts man as *totaliter aliter*, as the object of man's faith, is a God who is recognized by man as such in the scheme of man's epistemology of faith, and is not God himself as *totaliter aliter*. God as totally other can be truly other only in the dimension beyond human recognition or denial that God is totally other. This is the meaning of Emmanuel. In other words, Emmanuel is the *Urfaktum* that in no way comes within the field of vision of modern epistemology. Takizawa says that Barth's theology is not theocentric in the sense that it opposes the homocentrism of modern theology. God in Barth's theology is beyond the distinction between theocentrism and homocentrism, because both of these are man-made theological viewpoints. From this point of view, the theistic God, as the opposite to atheism, is not God as Emmanuel, and the criticism of theism from Zen Buddhism is not only right but also welcome from the Christian point of view. Understanding Barth in this way shows that Takizawa did not simply accept his theology, but adopted it, bringing it into line with Nishida's Self-identity of the Absolute Contradiction.

In Takizawa's opinion, Zen has something in common with Barthian theology on the level of the *Urfaktum* as Emmanuel. Before he went to

117

Europe to study under Barth, Takizawa had been interested in Nishida's philosophy, and it was Nishida who suggested that he should study under Barth. As has been briefly mentioned in the previous chapter in dealing with Yagi, Takizawa had criticized both Christianity, including Barth, and Zen Buddhism on the basis of his understanding of Emmanuel. Insofar as Emmanuel is the *Urfaktum*, which is beyond any reason and recognition given to it by man, it differs from the event in which Emmanuel was revealed and expressed in human history. According to Takizawa, Emmanuel was realized in Jesus as the prototype. However, the realization of Emmanuel in Jesus does not apply in the same way to Emmanuel itself, the *Urfaktum*. It is surely impossible to separate Jesus, in whom Emmanuel has for the first time been realized, from Emmanuel itself — in other words, Jesus Christ, the revealed Son of God. However, in Takizawa's opinion, these two are in principle quite distinct. If we say that God as the *Urfaktum* is the primary Emmanuel, then the realization of the *Urfaktum* in Jesus is the secondary Emmanuel. According to Takizawa, the order of the primary and secondary Emmanuel is never reversible, even though these two Emmanuels are inseparable, but at the same time not identical. In Takizawa's opinion, traditional Western Christianity, including Barth, has not recognized the distinction between the primary and secondary Emmanuel, nor their irreversible order, and has regarded the two as one and the same.

On the other hand, Takizawa also criticizes Zen, as advocated by Shin-ichi Hisamatsu (1889-1990), a well-known Zen leader, saying that Zen does not admit the irreversible priority of Emmanuel over everything else. Hisamatsu insists that we must kill Buddha. We can understand Buddha as *Hosshin*, the Ultimate Reality itself, only through Buddha as *Hohshin*, the manifestation and actualization of *Hosshin*. *Hohshin*, however, is not *Hosshin* itself, even though it may be true that man can understand *Hosshin* only through *Hohshin*. Therefore, we must kill and evacuate *Hohshin* in order to realize *Hosshin* itself. Tillich made a similar point when he said that the cross could be the cross, the revelation of God, only when it became transparent towards God; and that, consequently, it was no more necessary for the cross to remain as the cross. Furthermore, Meister Eckhart said that only when we made ourselves *geistlich arm*, "poor in spirit" (Matt. 5:3), and emptied our spirit that was looking for God, would the real God, who had not been involved in our vision and desire, manifest himself. According to Eckhart, it is right for such a God to be called Nothing; for this God is not an object of man's recognition, because man's spirit which seeks God has been emptied. In a famous sermon entitled "Durchbruch" (breakthrough), Eckhart said, "Gott ist ein nicht" (God is a Nothing). The similarity between Eckhart and Zen has often been pointed out. In any case, it is a logical necessity that the formless *Hosshin* or God as *niht* cannot have irreversible priority over the subject who is looking for *Hosshin* or *Got*. For insofar as we ascribe irreversible priority to *Hosshin* or *Got*, we are treating them as something objective, separating ourselves from them. Something inseparable, and at the same time unidentifiable, that is, something beyond the subject-object pattern of thought, cannot be an object to which we can give an attribute such as irreversible priority. Nevertheless, in Takizawa's opinion, the fact that Zen does not admit the irreversible priority of the *Urfaktum* makes Buddhist enlightenment a private affair.

To sum up, Takizawa interpreted Barth's *totaliter aliter* of God as *Urfaktum*, and insisted that the *Urfaktum* held an irreversible priority over human affairs, even though it is inseparable from and at the same time unidentifiable with them. Putting aside the problem whether Takizawa's understanding of Barth is right or wrong, we must admit that Takizawa did accept Barth's theology, bringing it into accord with the Oriental idea of Nothing. My view of Takizawa is that he seems to lack the ability to look at himself critically, in that the insistence on the irreversible priority of the *Urfaktum* is also Takizawa's insistence. Takizawa has no right to attribute such a property to the *Urfaktum*, insofar as the *Urfaktum* is beyond man's understanding. However, nobody will deny that Takizawa created the possibility of dialogue between Christianity and Buddhism, as well as a method for conducting it, by his very criticism of the two religions in terms of his understanding of Emmanuel.

Seiichi Yagi

In his first work, *The Formation of New Testament Thought* (1963), Seiichi Yagi (see pp. 99-101 above) examined the New Testament on the basis of the theological types he found within it. According to Yagi, we can find three themes in the New Testament: impersonality, individuality, and community. Jesus spoke of love, human life, and law, corresponding to these three themes respectively; and what Jesus ultimately wanted to express with these topics was, according to Yagi, the Reign of God. We can find parallels to these themes in the Primitive Church, which tried to express "Christ's work" by means of them. Yagi goes on to say that we must distinguish what Jesus called the "Reign of God" and what the Primitive Church called "Christ," from Jesus himself. In modern New Testament studies, the "Christ" of the Primitive Church has been distinguished from the "Jesus of history." Accepting this distinction, as well as the distinction made by Takizawa between the primary contact (Christ, according to Takizawa) and the secondary contact (the ideal realization of which is Jesus), Yagi further identified the "Reign of God" of Jesus with the "Christ" of the Primitive Church, i.e., the pneumatic, risen Christ who lived "in" the believers. "Christ" is thus another name for the reality that Jesus called the "Reign of God." Accordingly, Yagi attempted to explain how faith in the resurrection of Jesus developed as follows: After Jesus' death, his disciples became aware of the reality within them that he had called the "Reign of God." They interpreted this event as Jesus' epiphany in the manner of Matthew 4:16ff. People saw in Jesus the power of John the Baptist at work. Thus Yagi asserts that what Jesus called the "Reign of God" and what the Primitive Church called "Christ" were ultimately the same thing. Yagi calls this "order for integration." This is a reality that we can all realize, without presupposing God's special revelation in Jesus Christ, if we examine the content of religious enlightenment. This is somewhat reminiscent of Herbert Braun, who claimed that there was no difference in anthropology before and after the Easter faith, but that Christology was variable (*Die Sinn der neutestamentlichen Christologie,* 1957).

What Yagi meant by this "order for integration" was that man's way of being is like the pole of a magnet. The two poles of a magnet are different, but at the same time each one is indispensable to the other. The north pole cannot be the north pole by itself without the south pole, and vice versa. In this sense, we can say that the subject is identical with the object in the subject-object pattern. The field where the subject is identical with the object is the "Field of Integration." Love, the individual, and community will find their essential way of being in the Field. This is what Jesus called the Reign of God, and the kingdom of God is nothing but the fulfillment of this. Such a Field of Integration is fundamentally different from a field where one logic rules over everything rationally, i.e., the field of legalism. Yagi came to understand this by examining the New Testament itself. In *Jesus and Christ* (1969), he wrote that New Testament thought belongs to "the Field where subject is identical with object, if I understand it correctly." In other words, New Testament thought is different from modern thought based on the subject-object paradigm. In putting forward this type of thinking, Yagi had taken a step towards post-1970 theology.

Yagi claims to be able to translate this Integration into what Buddhism calls *engi* (mutual interaction) in *Contact Points between Buddhism and Christianity*, 1975. Knowing, as understood in the subject-object of modern epistemology, is replaced in Buddhism by *funbetsuchi* (knowing based on differentiation). Overcoming *funbetsuchi* means overcoming the presupposition of modern science that the only true knowledge of an object is that which is grasped by the subject. According to the idea underlying *engi*, however, everything exists in mutual interaction, and there is no foundation for giving a special status to the modern ego as the subject of knowledge, as *funbetsuchi* does. To live within the network of *engi* is to live within the Field of Integration. Yagi also thinks that if life within the Field of Integration is what the New Testament means, then the God of the New Testament in whom Jesus believed cannot be a personal God, as claimed by the Judeo-Christian tradition, but a God who is near the absolute Nothing beyond *funbetsuchi*. Buddhism and Christianity meet each other in this understanding of God (*Jesus and Nihilism*, 1979).

According to Yagi, it is the Transcendent that makes life in the Field of Integration possible for us. However, the Transcendent is not a subject that brings everything into order. It is something that does not exist in the same sense that things exist within the Field of Integration. The most fitting analogy to describe the Transcendent is "field." He writes that "when we express the Absolute (i.e., the Transcendent) as Field, the idea of Integration meets Nishida's philosophy" (*Contact*, p. 179). In Nishida's philosophy, subject is identical with object in the Field of the Self-identity of the Absolute Contradiction.[1] Yagi prefers the expression "the Transcendent"

---

1. For Nishida, *ba* (field) is not a spatial concept. It is, rather, the duality and simultaneity of the two poles in contradiction. I would have preferred "place" to "field" as a translation of *ba*, since the word "field" suggests a spatial entity to me. I use "field" as the translation of *ba* at Yagi's request.

to "the Field" because of his wish to preserve the transcendental dimension of the Absolute. Nishida's philosophy shows no understanding of the discontinuation between the Absolute and the Relative. As a consequence of this, Yagi thinks that Nashida has little sense of morality faced with the Absolute: "Sin and the individual's responsibility before God have no place in Nishida's philosophy." In Yagi's view, the Transcendent, understood as the Field of Reality, is reality as the activity to separate A and non-A, and at the same time to bind them. Therefore, it is Nothing, in the sense that there is an entity (*Where Can We Find God?*, 1977). In short, according to Yagi, Buddhism and Christianity meet each other in the idea of Integration, although Buddhism treats it as something like the ground of being, and Christianity treats it as something like the transcendent subject. However, it is the Transcendent that distinguishes Christianity from Buddhism. According to Yagi, the transcendental dimension is necessary to Christianity as the element for bringing the community of faith into unity. However, the transcendental dimension is comparatively rare in Buddhism.

Where I disagree with Yagi is in his understanding of the Field as the Transcendent, which confronts man with discontinuation, as explained above. Putting aside classical theological concepts such as human sin and responsibility before God, when the Transcendent is considered as Nothing, as he has said, he has no reason for calling the Field of Integration the Transcendent, distinguishing it from Nishida's understanding of the Field. Are not the concepts of the Field and the Transcendent incompatible with each other? I am afraid that Yagi still thinks of the Field of Integration as something like an entity, an object in the subject-object concept, side by side with the way he understands that the Field of Integration is the Field of Nothing, where the object is identical with the subject.

Yagi says that our authentic life has simultaneously a first-person relationship and a third-person relationship to the Absolute. To see the third person as the Absolute means that we are separated from the Absolute itself. However, only by making the Absolute the third person can we recognize it as such and speak *about* it. Making the Transcendent the third person and speaking about it with a common language is necessary, insofar as Integration forms a community. At this time, the Transcendent appears as "the confronted" to man, and will become the "Lord," while man will be aware of himself as a servant. Yagi confesses that "I am, after all, in the tradition of Christianity" in this kind of thinking (*The Falsehood of Ego and Religion*, 1980).

In his most recent book, *The Philosophy of Front-Structure* (1988), Yagi has developed his idea of Integration in terms of what he calls "Front-Structure." The fact that the north pole of a magnet cannot be a north pole without a south pole, and vice versa, means that the boundary field between the two poles belongs to both of the poles at the same time and in the same place. The boundary field is owned jointly by the two poles, so to speak. However, front presupposes rear, and everything consists of front and rear. In other words, by jointly owning the same field, the north and south poles can exist as the north and south pole respectively. This is the way of being for everything, and is not restricted to the poles of a magnet. This is also Yagi's explanation of *engi*. Moreover, according to Yagi, Front-Structure is applicable to our relation with the Transcendent vertically, not only to individual things horizontally. ("Horizontal" and "vertical" are Yagi's terms.) A community consisting of individual persons (or things) who are united by the Front-Structure to one another is merely what Yagi calls "order for integration," the biblical term for which is the "Reign of God." In Yagi's opinion, such a community is related to, or based upon, the Transcendent in the Front-Structure, understood vertically.

I do not think that a Transcendent of this sort is an entity, as far as the Front-Structure is an explanation of *engi*. Yagi is, in fact, one of those who have been most vigorous and explicit in their opposition to treating God as an entity, as an object of our recognition, that is to say, to treating God by *funbetsuchi*. However, a front presupposes a rear. There cannot be a front where there is no individual thing which is formed by the rear together with the front. Does not Yagi, then, think of the Transcendent as something like an individual thing, an entity, insofar as he speaks of the Front-Structure with reference to our relation to the Transcendent?

As I have shown above, Takizawa's and Yagi's theologies are motivated by what I have called the post-1970 *Zeitgeist*. Their theology has come near to the Buddhist idea of Nothing, as a consequence of their objections to the subject-object pattern of thought. Nevertheless, in my opinion, they kept remnants of this pattern, when Takizawa spoke of the irreversible priority associated with Emmanual, and when Yagi spoke of the Transcendent as the "Lord." Of course, we cannot expel the third person from the Field of Integration. If we do so, the Field of Integration

123

will become a false idea of integration. Masao Sekine asserts that God in the Old Testament is a pan*en*theistic God, in whom the Absolute Nothing is identical with the Absolute Being; consequently, it has a phase of the object, the third person. However, such a third person is by no means the Transcendent who confronts man with discontinuity and brings, as the Lord, a community of faith to unity. What brings a human community to unity is an idea or norm, not the order for integration.

The Theology of Religions

Yasuo Furuya

Another theology that has tried to break out of the "Barthian Captivity" is Yasuo Furuya's "theology of religions" (put forth in *The Theology of Religions,* 1985). In an age of pluralism like the present, in which various forms of a sense of values, including religious ones, have appeared, we cannot avoid the questions put to Christianity by other religions and attempts to answer them, assuming we accept the existence of other religions. However, Furuya finds it surprising that hardly anybody in Japan has so far undertaken an exercise of this sort.

One of the reasons for this lack is the influence of Barth's theology. As is well known, Barth insisted that there was a qualitative difference between God and man. In his view, we must make a distinction between faith and religion. Involvement in religion means being unfaithful, because religion is the work of humans. In other words, Barth was opposed to religions in general, since they are a human, not a divine, activity. For Barth, religion meant first of all Christianity. However, Japanese Barthians misunderstood this point and were inclined to think that for Barth "religion" meant non-Christian religions, while Christianity alone contained the truth. Consequently, they failed to see the need to be concerned with other religions. Moreover, according to Furuya, they made use of Barth's doctrine of the qualitative difference between God and man, and this led them to the understanding (or rather, misunderstanding), that faith was not concerned with the affairs of this world. This enabled them to avoid confronting the *Tenno* (Emperor) system, which had become a quasi-religion in the period before the Second World War. The so-called Barthian Captivity, then, was often the result of misunderstanding Barth.

The expression "theology of religions" appeared for the first time in the 1960s. The purpose of this theology is to hold dialogue with other religions (presupposing their existence), within the framework of the science of comparative religion, while at the same time maintaining the sole and absolute validity of God's revelation in Jesus Christ. In this sense, to use Toshio Sato's words, it is a theology of "compound eyes" (*The Loss and Restoration of Religion*, 1978). In Furuya's opinion, this was the situation in this country in the 1970s, once the Barthian Captivity was over. Takizawa's theology, which looked for mutual criticism between Buddhism and Christianity, and Yagi's theology, which tried to find the point of contact between the two, are products of the theology of religions (Furuya, *Theology of Religions*, pp. 115ff.). The problem of the theology of religions is how to maintain the absolute claims and the meaning of Christianity among other religions that also lay claim to absoluteness for themselves. In other words, it is carrying on the task that Ernst Troeltsch had tried to accomplish but left uncompleted.

Furuya's intention is to examine and evaluate other religions theologically, or in Barth's words, which he quotes, it is "eine theologische Würdigung der Religion und Religionen." However, this does not mean a return to the Barthian Captivity, which sees other religions with the closed vision of Christianity. Rather, it means seeking out some theological reality in other religions. This accords with H. Richard Niebuhr's view that exclusive faith in radical monotheism will paradoxically give birth to universal love, which cares not only for every human regardless of race and class, but even for one's enemy. This theology is also in agreement with that of Jürgen Moltmann, when he says that the more we concentrate exclusively on the cross, the more open our vision of other religions becomes. In Furuya's words, it is a theology in which "the exclusiveness of Revelation in Christ is not inconsistent with its comprehensiveness, and the uniqueness of Christ is not inconsistent with his universality" (*Theology of Religions*, pp. 333-35). In short, the theology Furuya sought is a theology which solves, and at the same time maintains, the contradiction between Christianity and other religions.

Furuya writes that his book *The Theology of Religions* should have been called *An Introduction to the Theology of Religions*. It is true that he ought to give further thought to developing the theology in which "Christ's uniqueness is not inconsistent with his universality." However, his idea of a theology in which the contradiction between exclusiveness and comprehensiveness, between uniqueness and universality, is understood without mutual conflict is in itself important enough. It seems to me that the assumption that lies hidden behind his suggested theology of religions cannot be anything other than the Self-identity of the Absolute Contradiction. There can be no third fixed position where the contradiction between two absolutely contradictory things, such as exclusiveness and comprehensiveness, uniqueness and universality, is brought together. In other words, Furuya knows that the theology of religions has as its goal a theology that cannot be constructed by modern rationalistic logic. Although Furuya does not seem to say so, one is seeking here God who cannot be an object of man's epistemology or of faith. The presupposition of the theology of religions, namely that there are many religions in the world besides Christianity, and the way in which it looks at Christianity from the viewpoint of religious pluralism, mean, as the other side of the coin, having to admit that Christianity is a relative, not an absolute, religion: one among many. This is the meaning of religious pluralism. However, on the other hand, nobody can admit that the religion he or she believes as a matter of life and death is a relative phenomenon. There is no faith without exclusiveness; and yet examination of one's own exclusiveness is the very stuff of the theology of religions. Its methodology cannot be other than the Self-identity of the Absolute Contradiction. And the Field of Self-identity of the Absolute Contradiction is Nothing.

Attempts to hold dialogue between Christianity and other religions have been a noticeable tendency of the theological mood of this country since 1970. The task of theology during the period of the Germanic Captivity was basically proclamation and mission, not dialogue. A theologian who engaged in dialogue with other religions, or even with philosophical thought, was often tacitly considered to lack confidence.[2] The Catholic Church in Japan has been taking part in dialogue with other religions more actively than the Protestant Church, even though, in the

2. However, to evaluate the similarities or parallelism between Buddhism and Christianity from the viewpoint of Christianity is not dialogue. In my opinion, Barth did not engage in dialogue with Buddhism when he wrote that it was God's *providentielle Fügung* that a religion such as *Jodo-shinshu* (a sect of Buddhism founded by Shinran) existed in Japan in the thirteenth century.

126

case of the Catholic Church, we must say "after the Second Vatican Council," rather than "after 1970." The fundamental attitude of the Catholic Church towards dialogue is, in the words of Jan van Bragt of Nanzan University, a Catholic university, "On the one hand, we must try to agree with the other by self-negation as far as possible. . . . On the other hand, however, this agreement will become possible only through serious confrontation and intermediation" (*Absolute Nothing and God*, 1981, pp. 8-9). In other words, self-negation and self-assertion, two contradictory attitudes, are both important. Besides the book quoted above, Nanzan University has published other books on interfaith dialogue which are the records of dialogue conferences attended by leading scholars of the religions concerned: *Religious Experience and Word: A Conversation between Buddhism and Christianity* (1978); *Shintoism and Christianity* (1984); *Esoteric Buddhism and Christianity* (1986); and *Tendai Buddhism and Christianity* (1988).

Masao Takenaka warns us that the present interest within the church in dialogue with other religions cannot always be considered as necessarily derived from the inner structure of Jesus' message, but seems to result more from the religious pluralism of the present age. Moreover, in his opinion, from the time of the Primitive Church onward, Christianity's encounter with other religions and with pagan cultures has been a confrontation, not dialogue. Present-day attempts at dialogue with other religions will fade away with the lapse of time, in his view, if the need for dialogue has not proceeded from the inner core of Jesus' message (*The Dialogue of Religions in the Modern Age*, 1979, p. 6). Takenaka is looking for the possibility of interfaith dialogue from a worldwide view.

Masatoshi Doi

Masatoshi Doi's method of doing theology is to examine "meaning" in theology (*Theology of Meaning*, 1963). According to Doi, meaning is realized when man adds his intention to an object. During the time of the Barthian Captivity in this country, Japanese theologians were working on the presupposition of the objective existence of God's revelation independent of man's existence. Doi writes in Bultmannian fashion: "Man's self-understanding, his understanding of his existence, i.e., the

Revelation, takes place only in relation to his faith. There is no revelation where there is no human faith" ("On Meaning," in *Mahayana Zen Buddhism*, No. 769, 1988, p. 7). Doi's emphasis on meaning in theological inquiry led to his interest in dialogue with other religions and the indigenization of Christianity in Japan. He is a leading member of the East-West Religions Project at the University of Hawaii. In Doi's view, human intention cannot be separated from one's own cultural background, which is not Christian. However, he does not agree with Tillich when he says that the present age is not an age of proclamation, but of dialogue. As Doi says, "I do not see that far ahead" ("On Theological Method," *Mahayana*, p. 26).

The fundamental problem in studying the theology of religions is how to acknowledge the relativity and pluralism of religions in the light of the absoluteness of the Christian message. What is needed is the simultaneous acceptance of completely contradictory attitudes, i.e., the relativity and the absolute claims of Christianity. Our faith presupposes the absolute validity of the Christian message. At the same time, however, we cannot deny the fact that there are many religions in the world. My view is that attempts to detect a third vision into which all religions will be subsumed, such as those of certain European and American scholars of religion, are not admissible. These attempts are in direct conflict with the absoluteness and exclusivity of religions. Those scholars who indulge in this kind of exercise show that they do not understand the reality of religion. The theology of religions cannot avoid the predicament involved in seeking universality from within specificity.

"Betweenness" and "Duality"

Furuya said that his *Theology of Religions* was meant as an introduction. What, then, is the main idea to be developed following this introduction? It must be the theology of meontology, whose characteristic is the "betweenness" of the contradiction, the contradiction between the absoluteness and relativity of Christianity. Whether Furuya would agree with this or not, meontological theology is, in my opinion, what Furuya suggested in his introduction. Takizawa and Yagi had tried to discover something by going beyond the contradiction. In other words, Takizawa tried to describe Emmanuel as the *Urfaktum;* Yagi, as the Transcendent. Yet there is another type of theology that maintains the "betweenness" of the contradiction.

Kazuo Muto

The consistent theme of Kazuo Muto's philosophy of religion has been, since the publication of his *Between Theology and the Philosophy of Religion* (1961), to investigate the "Betweenness" or the "Field" between the Christian faith and philosophical reason. Though he is an elder scholar of the Kyoto School, Muto has been concerned with this same issue or similar questions of post-1970 theology, anticipating the work of other theologians. In fact, the fundamental theme of his books *A New Possibility of the Philosophy of Religion* (1974) and *Theological and Philosophical Essays,* vols. 1 and 2 (1980-86) is the pursuit of the meaning of the "Betweenness" of the exclusivity of faith and the universality of philosophy.

According to Muto, the task of the philosophy of religion is to mediate between philosophy and theology. However, we cannot bring them into a unified order, because faith is by nature exclusive, while philosophy searches for the universal. Their unification would be possible only through some philosophical idea or theological dogma. A unification of this sort, however, runs counter to the task of the philosophy of religion. This suggests that Muto's philosophy of religion is pursuing a kind of mysticism, ultimately abandoning logical thinking. This is the difference between Muto on the one hand, and Takizawa and Yagionon on the other, who seem to have maintained their adherence to a completely logical way of thinking. The inclination towards mysticism is not restricted today to the philosophy of religion. Mysticism has been opposed by modern scientific thought, as well as by dialectical theology. However, we have now begun to realize the limits of human reason and the self-contradiction of scientific thought, especially since 1970. Consequently, the search has been for what is *ausserhalb* human reason and scientific thinking. Muto has gained insight into this contemporary world of thought by investigating the "Between" and the "Field" between faith and reason.

Muto has given expression to the "Between" as Religion A(?), applying Kierkegaard's terminology. Kierkegaard drew a distinction between

Religion A and Religion B, calling Religion A the universal religious reality, which can be the object of the philosophy of religion. Religion B, on the other hand, means faith in the paradox that a man called Jesus, who lived in human history, was the Christ, the Son of God. It is not a problem of truth, but of faith. Religion A and Religion B confront each other directly. Notwithstanding this, Muto asserts that Religion B does not, in a sense, disappear in Religion A, but is made complete in it (*The Philosophy of Religion*, 1955, pp. 135f.). It must be added that Religion A has nothing in common with a religious idea in an idealistic sense. The universal religious reality of Religion A means that "subjectivity is the truth," and it is this understanding that makes the religious stage different from the ethical stage. At the ethical stage, objectivity is the truth. In other words, the truth in Religion A is not concerned with objectivity, but with passion. Truth is objective uncertainty to which we cannot help passionately attaching ourselves. The reason why this religious standpoint is universal is that we can find the same understanding in other people, for example in Socrates.

In any case, this Kierkegaardian understanding of subjective truth foresees that truth itself will be superseded by another truth. (This can be contrasted with objective truth.) This means understanding that the standpoint itself will be denied and superseded. In other words, the inherent characteristic of Religion A is that its standpoint is not universally valid. This standpoint, that subjectivity is the truth, is denied by its inherent characteristic; and, conversely, the standpoint that subjectivity is the truth is actualized by the denial. This paradox is what Muto means by Religion A(?), or "Betweenness." This is religious universality after Religion B has passed through the denial of universality, and which therefore we cannot know in the rational scheme of knowledge. It is universality that lies in its non-being, so to speak. Insofar as each religion is confined to its own Religion B, there is no possibility of dialogue between religions. On the other hand, to compare religions on the level of Religion A, or by means of religious or philosophical ideas, as the comparative study of religions often does today, conflicts with the absoluteness of religion. Therefore, according to Muto, Religion A(?), which lies in its non-being, is immeasurably homologos with Self-identification of the Absolute Contradiction (*Philosophy of Religion,* p. 20). It is the "Field" between Religion A and Religion B, the essence of which is incompleteness and openness.

Muto often mentions Barth as an example of Religion B, suggesting that seeking Religion A(?) means leaving the Barthian Captivity. Muto has explained "Betweenness" in many ways. In the case of Kant, God is the Postulate of practical reason. However, if the Postulate means only an external supplement by which morality is to be completed, religion will become something like an appendix to morality, and there is no essential relation between morality and religion. According to Muto, however, the Postulate of practical reason has double meaning. That is to say, God is transcendent for pure reason, but not for practical reason. For if God is transcendent for practical reason, God cannot be the Postulate. God is in this sense *innerhalb der Grenzen der Vernunft*, and inherent in practical reason. Muto writes that the true meaning of Kant's philosophy of religion is that "the duality that what is postulated (i.e., God) is both inherent in, and at the same time transcendent to the postulate of practical reason" (*Theological and Philosophical Essays,* vol. 2, p. 44). In Muto's opinion, Kant's *Die Religion innerhalb der Grenzen der bloßen Vernunft* is the field where *die Religion ausserhalb der Grenzen der Vernunft* comes within the field of vision. It is the field of "Betweenness" or duality, of *innerhalb* and *ausserhalb* of human reason. We cannot point out and identify the field as such. Referring to Kant's opposition to the cosmological argument for God, found in his *Kritik der reinen Vernunft*, Muto describes the field as "the abyss" of man's reason. We can only know it through *docta ignorantia* with a recognition of the limit of human understanding. Therefore, it is present everywhere and at every time in the human world. This field is nothing but Religion A(?).

It should be noted here that one of the two poles which form the "Betweenness" — that is, the pole confronting reason and philosophy — is outside the scope of man's knowing. Therefore, "Betweenness" includes the other pole which forms the "Betweenness" itself. This is the meaning of "Betweenness." It will never become self-evident to human understanding. We cannot identify "Betweenness" in the same way that we can point out a valley between two mountains. What we can identify is an identity, not "between." It is evident that "Betweenness" of this kind has a kinship with mysticism and the idea of Nothing. In mysticism as *unio mystica,* we cannot separate ourselves from the pole confronting us while it continues to do so.

Muto himself has admitted the influence of Nishida's philosophy on his own thought. In his view, "Betweenness" becomes "The Field of Nothing" in Nishida's terminology, i.e., the "Field" of Self-identity of the Absolute Contradiction. He goes on to say that the same thing is said of the kingdom of God in the New Testament. In the kingdom of God, we are at the same time united with and confronted by God (*Theological and Philosophical Essays*, vol. 2, p. 6).

In short, Muto continues to use non-closed words such as "Betweenness," "Religion A(?)," "mystery," and "Nothing," and does not go beyond these concepts, as Takizawa and Yagi have tried to do. In this way Muto remains free from the Barthian Captivity and can be regarded as a post-1970 thinker. What is expressed in the terms "Betweenness," "the Field of Nothing," and the "kingdom of God" is the way of being of God and of the Absolute, who are, by their very nature, beyond positivistic, man-made religions, and also beyond the distinction between philosophy and theology. Such a God is *ausserhalb* the distinction between thought and religion, the East and the West. In a sense, what is required here is the "dereligionization" of Christianity, which is also a characteristic of theology after 1970.

Masaya Odagaki

While Muto, as a philosopher of religion, has sought the "Betweenness" of religion and philosophy, Masaya Odagaki, as a theologian, has pursued the "Duality" of faith and reason, of belief and unbelief. Odagaki was the first theologian in this country to insist that the absolute Nothing is a suitable way of expressing God (*Hermeneutical Theology*, 1975). Like Muto, Odagaki does not try to move beyond the "Betweenness," because he thinks that the total otherness of God is beyond the grasp of any human idea, and that the "Betweenness" or the "Duality" between being and non-being is the only way of being a *totaliter aliter* God. In this sense, epistemologically speaking, God does not exist; that is, God is Nothing.

We can find the suggestion of similar ideas in Barth and Tillich, and opposition to considering God as an object lies behind both the death of God theology and liberation theology. This kind of thinking has its own reasons, which are theologically necessary. However, it is true that the idea that God is Nothing appears anti-Christian to conventional Christianity. In particular, the reaction to this kind of theological thinking from churches with a short tradition, such as the Japanese church, is often hysterical. The reason that two theological schools were closed down during the time of university disturbances, as related above, was basically that our conventional Japanese church was so weak that she could not stand up to what we call radical theology. However, the main thrust of Odagaki's argument is non-theism, that is, that we cannot know God as an object. In other words, he argues in favor of panen-theism, not atheism in Nietzsche's sense of negating the God of theism.

Odagaki says that Jesus became Christ by a language-event. Accord-ing to Heidegger, language is the "call of being" and "the illuminating-concealing arrival of being itself." Language is the *Unterschied* between being itself and a being (or entity). Being is *das Anwesen des Anwesenden* in language. In other words, being has by nature a dual character. Being of this sort, with its twofold character, is Nothing seen from the view-point of entity. This Nothing, however, is not nothing as the negation of an entity, but Nothing which lets an entity (and accordingly the negation of entity) exist. To use Nishida's terminology, it is the absolute Nothing. Jesus was the Revelation of God because Jesus' words were a language-event and the illuminating-concealing arrival of God. It is appropriate to regard such a kind of God as Nothing. This double way of being is, as I have repeatedly explained, the very way of being of the absolute as the *totaliter aliter*. According to Odagaki, it is meaningless to inquire into the relationship between God and being, because the language-event treats what is beyond man's distinctions and compari-sons (*Hermeneutical Theology*, p. 327). A theological assertion of this nature would not be possible without the influence of Gerhard Ebeling, Ernst Fuchs, and especially Martin Heidegger. There is a linguistic philosophy within Oriental thought to the effect that language is not simply a vehicle for conveying concepts, but allows reality to exist. Koan of Zen is a good illustration of this.

In Odagaki's view, the duality of the opposites — being and entity, God and man, the absolute and the relative — that Muto described as "Betweenness" had also been pointed out by Nicholas of Cusa, Meister Eckhart, and Plotinus, as well as by Lao-tsze and Chuang-tsze (*To an Unknown God*, 1980). Opposition and distinction occur only in human knowledge, and so the distinction between Oriental and Western thought is deprived of its meaning in the field of duality, which is beyond distinction. Theologically speaking, faith is the dual condition of belief and unbelief. Luther's *simul justus et peccator* should be understood not only in an ethical sense, but also in an epistemological sense, as Tillich once said. German mysticism said that the true God is *Gott über Gott.* However, in Odagaki's opinion this does not mean that there is the true God behind God as the object of our knowing, but that God is the duality of presence and absence (*Philosophical Theology,* 1983).

The absolute is the duality of the absolute and the relative. The absolute confronting the relative is not absolute, because it depends on the relative as the object of the confrontation. In the same way, God is the duality of God and man. This condition suggests that the absolute consists of three elements: the absolute, the relative, and the duality of the absolute and the relative. Similarly, God consists of three elements: God, man, and the duality of God and man. According to Odagaki, this is the meaning of the doctrine of the Trinity. The duality is just what the Holy Spirit means (*God in Contemporary Thought,* 1988). It is clear that Nishida's philosophy lies behind this kind of thinking.

Indigenization

Post-1970 theology in Japan has liberated itself from the Germanic Captivity, as we have outlined above. It is in this period that theological thinking of our own, not just the investigation and study of European and American theology, developed. In other words, the conditions under which the indigenization of Christianity in this country can be undertaken meaningfully have at last come into being. The indigenization of Christianity is probably a problem peculiar to our country, for when Christianity was introduced, Japan already had highly sophisticated religions and philosophy. Protestant Christianity, in contrast, has a history of only one hundred years in Japan. To attempt to evaluate the Japanese church and theology by directly applying the standards of European Christianity, as Ishihara and Kumano did, is in my opinion a sterile exercise.

The theory of indigenization has changed remarkably since 1970. Kiyodo Takeda classified five types of indigenization: the buried type (being buried and lost through compromise); the isolation type (isolation refusing compromise); the confrontation type; the grafting type (fusion maintaining confrontation in the background); and the apostasy type (seeking for indigenization paradoxically through apostasy). It appears that these are the only possible ways open when Christianity, as a positivistic religion, tries to adapt to another culture without reforming or metamorphosing itself. Takeda herself adopts the grafting approach, in which Christianity should confront Japanese indigenous culture by burying itself in and being fused into the Japanese soil, while at the same time maintaining a posture of confrontation, as suggested by the parable of the grain of wheat ("The Task and Method of Receiving Christianity: Concerning the Thought of Inazo Nitobe," in *The Method and Object of the History of Thought: Japan and Europe*, ed. K. C. Takeda, 1961). In this classification, however, confrontation between Christianity and Japanese religions serves as an underlying assumption and a background against which other approaches are classified.

On the other hand, religious pluralism, as advocated by John Hick, John Cobb Jr., and W. C. Smith, has problems of its own. In the first place, religious pluralism is a denial of the absoluteness claimed by each religion. It therefore contains an element of denial of religion itself, for there is no religion that does not make exclusive absolute claims. The theology of religions inevitably led to opposition to Barthian Captivity; but on the other hand, it must equally oppose religious pluralism. Second, humans have no right, fundamentally speaking, to take a neutral position and to compare one religion with another. Faith is concerned with that which is beyond comparison. The comparative study of religions is an enterprise that does not touch religious life, i.e., faith. Dialogue between religions and the indigenization of Christianity will take place only when each religion is expected to metamorphose itself through self-negation in dialogue. However, the uniqueness and originality of a religion is not inconsistent with the metamorphosis of that religion through dialogue. Rather, to remain unchanged means that the religion sees itself as relative, since unchangeability has meaning only if it presupposes the existence of other entities, and sees itself as one among many.

Yohji Inoue

Yohji Inoue, a Catholic priest, has been trying to acculturate Christianity in this country, not against a background of confrontation as described by Takeda, but by presupposing a change in Christianity itself. This is

what I call the post-1970 theory of indigenization. During his eight years
as a monk within the Order of Our Lady of Mount Carmel in France,
he became aware of the profound difference between Japan and Europe.
For him, the foundation of the Western way of thinking is substance,
while the foundation of Japanese thinking is "the field which envelopes
substances." As for nature, while Europe's "culture of stone" confronts
nature, Japanese culture is "with nature." Therefore, any attempt to
transplant European Christianity, which presupposes substance, intact
to Japan cannot be successful. The metamorphosis of Christianity from
a religion of "substance" to a religion of "field" is necessary.

However, there is a way of seeing Christianity as a religion of "field."
As Inoue understands it, the God of Christianity is not a substantial
object of whom humans can speak standing outside God, but something
more like a field. When Jesus called upon God, saying *Abba*, God was
not a substance whom Jesus could see as an object, even though God
was the object of his prayer and calling. When an infant calls his father,
saying *Abba*, there is no clear distinction between the infant (the subject), and its father (the object). There is only a happy experience of
unity in love, in the field, so to speak. Inoue writes, "There was an
experience of unity in love beyond the subject-object concept in the
word 'abba,' when Jesus spoke this word and called to God" (*Japan and
Jesus' Face*, 1976). The important thing is the reality or the field, which
involves both subject and object. The framework in which Christianity,
the subject, confronts Japanese religion, the object of Christian religion,
must be nullified; and they must be unified in the "field" of love. This
is what Inoue seems to suggest. In any case, indigenization will be real
only where confrontation is overcome though the metamorphosis of
Christianity.

Discovering common or parallel elements in Catholic Christianity
and Japanese religion does not result in the indigenization of Christianity. Speaking from the viewpoint of Catholic Christianity, this can
only come about when God ceases to be an object enclosed within the
religion of Catholic Christianity and becomes the "field" beyond the
confrontation between Christianity and non-Christianity, between
being and non-being. In Inoue's words, God is "beyond the realm where
the distinction between being and non-being is meaningful" and "God
is something which cannot become an object of our recognition by any
means." In other words, "God is One who manifests Himself in Nothing.

In this sense, we can say that God is the Field of Nothing" (*Japan and Jesus' Face*, p. 78). It is clear that Inoue's understanding of God is meontological and thus is characteristic of post-1970 theology.

In short, Inoue maintains that we must return to the religion of the "field," as advocated by Jesus himself, rejecting the religion of "substance" of traditional Western European Christianity. Inoue expresses his sympathy with the theology of the Eastern Church, especially with that of Vladimir Lossky, who maintained that God was beyond any kind of confrontation and opposition among individuals, even the opposition between being and non-being, and that in this sense God was something like a "field." In Inoue's opinion, the indigenization of Christianity in Japan will be possible only when European Christianity penetrates to the level of the religion of the "field" that lies beneath its religion of "substance." In other words, it is only through the metamorphosis of the Christianity of the Western world that indigenization of Christianity in Japan, whose ways of thinking are based originally on the "field," not on "substance," will be possible. This kind of metamorphosis means, in a sense, the self-negation of Western traditional Christianity. However, wasn't this self-negation originally an element in Jesus' crucifixion?

Shusaku Endo

The idea that self-negation on the part of Christianity is necessary for its mission to be successful has also been put forward by Shusaku Endo, a Catholic novelist. His basic understanding of Christianity seems to be that humanity can realize God only through God's absolute silence, and Christ only through the tragic death of Jesus on the cross. A person who is living in the shadow can suggest light only by describing the darkness of shadow. Humans are not living in a place from where they can see both shadow and light. In a pamphlet attached to his book *On the Dead Sea* (1973), Endo says that if a writer tries to portray the holy, it will necessarily become grotesque since the holy, as grasped by human understanding, is a distortion. In short, humanity cannot know real God within a religion. Therefore, if it is at all possible for humans to realize God and Christ, it can only be through God's silence and Jesus' death. Accordingly, the negation of a religion called Christianity is necessary in order that God may be realized by humanity. Endo's standpoint is nearer to *theologia crucis* than to the Catholic point of view. In all of this, Christianity is not regarded as a religion enclosed within human vision.

If Christianity wants to become indigenous in non-Christian countries, metamorphosis through self-negation is necessary. The mission that does not anticipate this is haughty by nature, no matter how humble its attitude may appear towards indigenous religions. Mission must not be the conquest of other religions. The cross itself is the most striking self-negation. However, self-negation must not be surrender of the self. The problem of the theology of mission lies in this predicament.

Historical Consciousness

A new awareness of the history of Christianity in modern Japan — in other words, a new understanding of Christianity in modern Japan — has also taken place since 1970. This historical consciousness insists that it is meaningless to evaluate the history of Christianity in Japan by the standard of European and American Christianity, and that there must be a history of Japanese Christianity written out of our own historical necessity. This is another example of an exodus of Japanese theology from the Germanic Captivity.

It was the church conflict that took place around 1970 that led to the demand for a new historical perspective. Akio Dohi has said in the postscript to his *History of Japanese Protestant Christianity* (1980) that we cannot treat this age of great turmoil apart from the mainstream of the history of Christianity in Japan. We must, in the first place, look closely at the actual situation of the Japanese church, as revealed in this period of turmoil. Then, writes Dohi, "the history of Christianity after 1970 must be written by describing the course of events during the turmoil and by making their meaning clear" (p. 459). Dohi does not agree with Ishihara in his criticism of the Japanese church by taking the history of European Christianity as his model. Dohi writes, "the history of Japanese Christianity must be forged within its own context," however immature it may be (*Essays on the History of Japanese Protestant Christianity*, 1987, p. 15). We can safely say that another kind of historical awareness, different from Ishihara's, has developed in this country.

Confronting the Tenno (Emperor) system of government has been one of the main themes of the Christian church in Japan for the past one hundred years (Arimichi Ebisawa and Saburo Ohuchi, *History of Christianity in Japan,* 1970, pp. 139 and 141). What is known as the issue of blasphemy towards the emperor on the part of Kanzo Uchimura has been touched upon in chapter 1. However, there is also an example of the opposite behavior. In 1942, the year following the formation of the United Church of Christ in Japan, as the result of pressure from the Japanese government, the moderator of the United Church of Christ in Japan visited the Ise Shrine, the principal shrine of Shintoism, and worshiped there, informing Amaterasu-Ohmikami, a goddess and the original ancestor of Tenno, of the formation of the United Church. It is difficult to find a similar example in the whole history of Christianity. Behind this pathetic event lay the Barthian Captivity and a poor misunderstanding of Barth's theology.

Another difficult problem facing the present-day Japanese church is the Yasukuni Shrine. This was, until the end of the Second World War, a government-run shrine of Shintoism, dedicated to all the people killed in the war. This shrine is rather like a non-religious Tomb of the Unknown Warrior. Since the Second World War, it has become in legal terms a "religious institution," following the policy of the separation of government and religion. However, since 1969 there has been a persistent political movement aiming to restore government control again, thus violating the principle of the separation of government and religion, one of the most fundamental principles of the modern civil society. So far this movement has been blocked, mainly through objections by Christians and Buddhists (Nanzan University, ed., *Shintoism and Christianity,* 1984; Masahiro Tomura, *Japanese Fascism and the Problem of the Yasukini Shrine,* 1974).

In dealing with the Tenno system and Shintoism, the religion which is inseparable from Tenno, in relation to the indigenization of Christianity in Japan, the most important task is to determine our viewpoint. I have the impression that Christianity in Japan has, on the whole, put off considering this problem, giving only vague answers to the question of confrontation, though we have had exceptions on both sides of the argument. However, freedom of faith within a modern civil society suggests that we must regard our own faith as relative (and at the same time as absolute). This is simply the problem of the theology of religions.

If we are unaware of the relativity of our own religion, opposition to the Tenno system as a quasi-religion and to the problem of the Yasukuni Shrine will become something like a see-saw reflecting the ups and downs of religious superiority. Which is better, Christianity or Shintoism? This kind of question is not only fruitless and impossible to answer, but it also runs counter to our standpoint. The answer will be given by the metamorphosis and self-negation of Christianity — surely, not only the metamorphosis of Christianity, but of every religion, that is, by the meontological theology that is characteristic of post-1970 theology.

*   *

IN CLOSING THIS CHAPTER, I want to put a question to Western readers of the present book. I have consistently argued in this chapter that traditional Western Christianity needs to undergo its own metamorphosis through self-negation by becoming meontological Christianity. I have also asked whether this was not the meaning of *theologia crucis*. How, then, does your theology respond to this point of view?

Epilogue

IT WAS A COINCIDENCE that at the time when all four of these chapters were written, Japan entered into a new period through the death of Emperor Showa in January 1989. It was, however, quite symbolic that the most recent theology to appear after the death of the emperor, a theology which dramatically demonstrated that Shintoistic Japan was unchanged, was a "theology of Japan." A book with this title, *Theology of Japan*, co-authored by Yasuo Furuya and Hideo Ohki, was a call for a theology that would make Japan its object.

According to the authors, the theology of Japan is not a Japanese theology. The word *of* in the title indicates not the genitive but the accusative case; thus it indicates the object, Japan. This theology questions Japan, totally and radically, from a theological point of view. The theology of Japan is a theology that pursues the question of what Japan is. It is probable that this kind of theology has never been proposed or attempted in the history of Christian theology.

The book is divided into two parts. The first part, written by Furuya, is a historical study of the relationship between Japan and Christianity. History clearly shows that Japan is not an abstract problem for Christianity. On the other hand, neither is Christianity an abstract problem for Japan. They have been formidable opponents of each other. This was the reason that Japan expelled Roman Catholic missionaries, forbade Christianity, and in the seventeenth century closed the country to the West for more than two hundred years. When Japan was forced to open the country to the West in the nineteenth century, the government invented a new religion in order to prevent the spread of Christianity. This new religion was State Shinto, based on emperor worship. On the other hand, Christians were persecuted during the closed period to such an extent that they could survive only as "hidden Christians," whose beliefs became merged with those of Buddhism and Shinto. Even after the onset of modernization, Christians remained under the control of State Shinto, so that they were unable to resist militarism and war and were forced to obey and collaborate. To be sure, after defeat in World War II, and under the new constitution which was influenced by Western ideas of democracy and human rights, Christianity has enjoyed much more freedom than ever before. However, Christianity still remains a small minority — about one percent of the population. Why is this so?

Furuya supports what Hendrik Kraemer said of postwar Japan, which seems to have undergone a change, in these words:

> After the American Occupation, when Japan had to start afresh with a clean slate and learn the "democratic way," under American pressure, the Emperor disavowed his "divinity," and State Shinto was abolished. It would, however, be all too naive to think that by this disavowal on the radio the Emperor had altered anything in the hearts of the Japanese, as to his real pivotal position in the Japanese "hierarchical way." He remains the sacred inviolable Chief, exempt from all criticism. . . . Yet it will be wise to reckon with the fact that Japan's spiritual core has not changed. . . . Shinto will continue to enshrine the real soul of Japan. (*World Cultures and World Religion,* 1960, pp. 225, 226)

What happened around the time of the emperor's death in 1989 was merely the confirmation of what Kraemer had observed and predicted thirty years ago. Furuya pointed out even before the death of the emperor, however, that the real problem of Christianity in Japan was Japan itself, whose spiritual core is a Shintoistic way of thinking and living, with the emperor as its peak. This is why we need a theology of Japan. The spiritual core of Japan is so powerful that even Christians in Japan are not free from its control. It is no wonder that during wartime most Japanese Christians supported the war and ultranationalism. They were unable to relativize Japan or to criticize nationalism. What Japanese

Christians need, not only for themselves, but for Japan and for the world, is to have a point of view by which they can transcend ethnocentric and self-righteous nationalism.

The task of theology in Japan is not just to criticize Japan and nationalism, but to clarify Japan's mission as a nation and to help nationalism achieve its purpose. According to Furuya, Japan's mission is to be a "peace nation," as the postwar constitution declares. This constitution is a unique and, one might say, a most Christian-like constitution. Why and how did Japan adopt such a constitution, in which Japan declared that she would never wage war again?

Having studied the history of Japan in relation to Christianity, Furuya believes that it was providential. If Japan had not been defeated, she would not have this peace constitution. To use the common expression in Japan, by "the baptism of the atomic bomb" the old militant Japan died and a new peace-making generation was born. Japan's mission, therefore, is to become a peace-making nation in today's world, which is threatened by nuclear war. Thus the task of the Japanese church is not only to criticize, but to be responsible to Japan, so that Japan may be faithful to her mission. Furuya then calls the Japanese church to her mission in the proper sense, namely the evangelization of Japan. Unless Christians comprise at least ten percent of the population, the church cannot fulfill her task effectively as "the salt of the earth" and "the light of the world." The evangelization of Japan is one application of the theology of Japan.

The second part of the book, written by Ohki, is a discussion of methodological questions relating to the theology of Japan. By the very fact of its being a theology, its basic viewpoint is that of God, which one should adopt in dealing with Japan. Ohki, however, rejects the idea of dealing with Japan on the basis of the doctrine of creation, in the way that "German theology," for example, attempted to do in the work of Friedrich Gogarten. In order to deal with Japan theologically, Ohki proposed a method called "theological relativism." This is derived from prophetic thought structure, as spoken by Amos in the Old Testament (9:7-8).

Out of theological relativism comes a historical world perspective by which all races and nations are seen as *relative* under *God*. In this theology God is no longer the God of a nation, such as Israel, but transcends all nations. Here also, the human point of view is negated, and God's point of view is established. The understanding of revelation in theological relativism is much wider than Barth's. Theology here takes on the character of historical theology. It enables us to make Japan a theme of theology, not merely on the basis of the doctrine of creation within dogmatics, but from a historical perspective in historical theology. The theology of Japan is, therefore, first of all, a radicalization of theology, which approaches Japan from God's point of view; and second, it is a task of historical theology par excellence. This is not derived from Barth's theology. Accordingly, says Ohki, unless theology is equipped afresh with a new methodology, Japan cannot become a theme of theology.

The theology of Japan is different from the so-called Japanese theology, such as Kitamori's theology of the pain of God. It is concerned not only with Japan's participation in the formation of theology, but primarily with the Japanese themselves, who are supposed to participate in theological formation. In other words, the theology of Japan must deal with the problem of the subjectivity of the Japanese. As Karl Löwith pointed out, "The Japanese are all patriots" who love themselves as they are, without any "European" self-criticism. Löwith's criticism also applies to Japanese Christians. As Furuya says in the first part of the book, the problem is not only with Japan, the object of the theology of Japan, but with Japanese Christians, the subject of the theology of Japan. For Japanese Christians themselves could not relativize and criticize Japanese nationalism and patriotism before and during the war. Here again, in order to deal with the question of subjectivity, theological relativism is needed.

The theology of Japan, however, is more positively concerned with establishing a theological existence as one of its theological subjects. What, then, is the *topos,* or place, where such theological existence can be formed? After discussing the "Japanese heart" of Norinaga Motoori, a Shinto scholar of the eighteenth century, and the *topos* of Kitaro Nishida, a Buddhist philosopher of the twentieth century, Ohki concludes by saying:

"The theology of Japan" is made possible by the establishment of *theological* existence through "conversion," and at the *topos* of theological existence provided by the "event of resurrection." That "topos" is the "Church." In that sense, the "theology of Japan" is

Church theology, whose *Sitz* is the "Church." The theme of Church theology is, of course, "God," who revealed Himself in Jesus Christ. In speaking of this "God" (= theo-logia), we self-consciously place our own being under the absolute God through theological relativism, on the basis of which we question "Japan." (*Theology of Japan,* pp. 269f.)

In the preface to a recent issue of *Theological Studies in Japan* (No. 28, 1989), Furuya appeals to members of the Japan Society of Christian Studies to address the task of the theology of Japan. Reactions to this appeal are yet to be seen. There is no doubt, however, that since the idea of the theology of Japan has now been proposed and published, theology in Japan is just beginning to turn its attention to its own theological task, instead of merely studying European and American theology.

The fact that this present work, the first book on the history of Japanese theology, has been written by Japanese theologians is a sign of this change of direction. The history of Japanese theology is an indispensable theme of the theology of Japan. In this sense, this book is one of the first products of this theology. It does not mean, however, that there should be only one theology of Japan. Even in this book, several theologies of Japan are represented. The description of each chapter reflects each writer's theology. Since this book has been written by more than one author, readers may not find a unified interpretation, but rather different interpretations of the history of theology in Japan. But as this book shows, Christianity in Japan has always been very diverse, even from the beginning. Christianity and Japan present each other with complex problems.

We hope that this first history of Japanese theology, written by Japanese, may not only interest readers in other countries, but also help them to understand Japan and Christianity in Japan. Japan's existence and worldwide influence cannot be overlooked in the world today. At the same time, this means that Japan is a problem both for the world and for Christianity today. In spite of, or because of, its modernization and Westernization, Japan is a country in which Christians are still a small minority of the population. This means that Christianity is also a problem for Japan.

The theology of Japan is therefore not only significant and necessary for Japanese Christianity and church, but also for world Christianity and church. For when Japanese theologians face the task of the theology of Japan, they must inevitably face the task of the theology of the world. The theology of Japan, though this may sound paradoxical, is destined to be an ecumenical theology. The more Japanese theologians engage in the theology of Japan, the more they may be involved in the ecumenical tasks of the church and theology.

The basic reason that Japanese theologians have so far not contributed much to Christian theology on a world scale is not just the language barrier, but rather their theological stance. However, as the history of Japanese theology shows, they have studied and learned from Western theology to such an extent that they now feel ready to cope with the theology of Japan and of the world.

This may provide one answer to a question some readers of this book might have had. One Japanese theologian's name, which is quite familiar in the ecumenical world but which has so far not appeared in this book, is Kosuke Koyama (1929-). Since the publication of his *Waterbuffalo Theology* (1974), Koyama has been regarded as a representative Japanese theologian. Unfortunately, however, his contribution to theology in Japan is almost nil. This may be due to the fact that he has been working outside Japan for so long, and that he has been writing for and addressing non-Japanese Christians. On the other hand, it may also be due to the fact that until recently Japanese theologians have not been interested in the theology of Japan. Now, however, because they are beginning to cope with the new task in which they make Japan an object of theology, they might be interested in Koyama's point of view. Having lived abroad for many years, he has been looking at Japan as an object from the outside, and has been engaged in a sort of theology of Japan, without using the term, as shown by his *Mount Fuji and Mount Sinai* (1984).

Finally, we would like to come back to the two questions raised in the introduction. The first was whether or not we have come of age, so that we are able to write a history of Japanese theology. The second was whether there was, in fact, a "Japanese theology." As we said there, we would like to know readers' answers and reactions. Whatever your answers may be, we hope that we Japanese theologians may engage in dialogue with you, in order to deal with our share of the common tasks of the church and theology in the world today. At the least, we hope that this volume will help you to understand our theological situation and history, which is necessary for fruitful dialogue.

Contributors

AKIO DOHI is professor of church history at the School of Theology, Doshisha University, Kyoto. He has studied at the School of Theology, Doshisha University, and Union Theological Seminary, New York. He is an ordained minister of Kyodan (United Church of Christ in Japan).

YASUO FURUYA is chaplain and professor of theology and religion at the International Christian University, Tokyo. He was educated at Tokyo Union Theological Seminary, San Francisco Theological Seminary, Tübingen University, and Princeton Theological Seminary (Th.D.). He has also been concurrently pastor of the International Christian University Church.

MASAYA ODAGAKI is professor of religion at Kunitachi College of Music, Tokyo. He was educated at the School of Theology, Aoyama Gakuin University, Tokyo, and Drew University (Ph.D.). He is a licensed minister of Kyodan.

TOSHIO SATO is professor of systematic theology at Tokyo Union Theological Seminary, Tokyo. He was educated at Tokyo Union Theological Seminary, Union Theological Seminary, New York, and Hartford Theological Seminary (Ph.D.). He has also been pastor of Nakamurabashi Church, Tokyo, of Kyodan.

SEIICHI YAGI is professor of philosophy and ethics at Toin University, Yokohama. He studied at Tokyo University and Göttingen University, and received a D.Litt. from Kyushu University.

Bibliography

Akaiwa, Sakae, *Exodus from Christianity* (Kirisutokyō Dasshutsuki), 1964.

Arai, Sasagu, *Commentary on the of Acts of Apostles* (Shitogyōden), vol. 1, 1977.

———, *Jesus and His Age* (Iesu to sono Jidai), 1974.

———, *Jesus Christ* (Iesu Kirisuto), 1979.

———, *Primitive Christianity and Gnosticism* (Genshi Kirisutokyō to Gunō-sisushugi), 1971.

Ariga, Tetsutarō, *The Problems of Ontology in Christian Thought* (Kirisutokyō Shisō ni okeru Sonzairon no mondai), 1969.

———, *A Study of Origen* (Origenesu Kenkyū), 1943.

———, *Symbolical Theology* (Shōchōteki Shingaku), 1946.

——— (with Tadakazu Uoki), *An Outline of the History of Christian Thought* (Gaisetsu Kirisutokyō Shisōshi), 1934.

Asano, Junichi, *The Book of Job* (Yobuki), 1968.

———, *Commentary on the Book of Job* (Yobuki Chūkai), 4 vols., 1965-74.

———, *Interpretation of Some Psalms* (Shihen Senshaku), 1933.

———, *Moses* (Mōse), 1980.

———, *The Old Testament Bible* (Kyūyaku Seisho), 1939.

———, *Psalms* (Shihen), 1972.

———, *Some Problems of Old Testament Theology* (Kyūyaku Shingaku no Shomondai), 1941.

———, *Study of Israelite Prophets* (Isuraeru Yogensha no Kenkyū), 1955.

———, *Study of the Book of Job* (Yobuki no Kenkyū), 1962.

———, *Study of the Prophets* (Yogensha no Kenkyū), 1931.

Dohi, Akio, *Essays on the History of Japanese Protestant Christianity* (Nihon Purotesutanto Kirisutokyōshi Shiron), 1987.

————, *History of Japanese Protestant Christianity* (Nihon Purotesutanto Kirisutokyōshi), 1980.

Doi, Masatoshi, *Theology of Meaning* (Imi no Shingaku), 1963.

Ebina, Danjō, *The Essence of Christianity* (Kirisutokyō no Hongi), 1903.

Furuya, Yasuo, *Theology of Religions* (Shūkyō no Shingaku), 1985.

————, and Hideo Ohki, *Theology of Japan* (Nihon no Shingaku), 1989.

Hatano, Seiichi, *The Essence and the Basic Problems of Philosophy of Religion* (Shūkyōtetsugaku no Honshitsu oyobi sono Konponmondai), 1920.

————, *Introduction to the Philosophy of Religion* (Shūkyōtetsugaku Joron), 1940.

————, *The Origin of Christianity* (Kirisutokyō no Kigen), 1908.

————, *Philosophy of Religion* (Shūkyōtetsugaku), 1935.

————, *Time and Eternity* (Toki to Eien, orig. in English). 1943.

Hino, Masumi, *History of Christian Doctrine* (Kirisutokyō Kyōrishi), 1917.

Ikeda, Yutaka, *The World of the Old Testament* (Kyūyakuseisho no Sekai), 1982.

Imai, Toshimichi, *Old Testament Theology* (Kyūyaku Seisho Shingaku), 1911.

Inoue, Yohji, *Japan and Jesus' Face* (Nihon to Iesu no Kao), 1976.

Ishihara, Ken, *The Development of Christianity* (Kirisutokyō no Tenkai), 1972.

————, *History of Christianity* (Kirisutokyōshi), 1934.

————, *Philosophy of Religion* (Shūkyō Tetsugaku), 1915.

————, *Schleiermachers Reden über die Religion* (Schleiermacher no Shūkyōron), 1922.

————, *The Source of Christianity* (Kirisutokyō no Genryū), 1972.

Ishii, Jiro, *A Study of Schleiermacher* (Schleiermacher Kenkyū), 1948.

Iwashita, Soichi, *Augustine's "City of God"* (Augustinusu 'Kami no Kuni'), 1935.

————, *The Deposit of Faith* (Shinkō no Isan), 1941.

————, *Medieval Current of Thought* (Chūsei Shichō), 1928.

————, *Neo-Scholastic Philosophy* (Shin Sukora Tetsugaku), 1932.

————, *The Study of the History of Medieval Philosophical Thought* (Chūsei Tetsugakushisōshi Kenkyū), 1942.

Kan, Enkichi, *The Basic Concepts of the Philosophy of Religion* (Shūkyōtetsugaku no Kisogainen), 1930.

————, *Modern Philosophy of Religion* (Gendai no Shūkyōtetsugaku), 1934.

————, *Reason and Revelation* (Risei to Keiji), 1953.

————, *Religious Revival* (Shūkyō Fukkō), 1934.

————, *A Study of Karl Barth* (Kāru Baruto Kenkyū), 1968.

————, *A Study of the Theology of Barth* (Baruto Shingaku no Kenkyū), 1979.

————, *The Theology of Barth* (Baruto no Shingaku), 1939.

————, *The Turning of Christianity and Its Principle* (Kirisutokyō no Tenkō to sono Genri), 1930.

Kashiwai, En, *History of Christianity* (Kirisutokyōshi), 1924.

————, *Short History of Christianity* (Kirisutokyō Shōshi), 1909.

Kida, Kenichi, *Service and Writings of the Israelite Prophets* (Isuraeru Yogensha no Shokumu to Bungaku), 1976.

Kitamori, Kazoh, *The Theology of the Pain of God* (Kami no Itami no Shingaku), 1946.

Koyame, Kosuke, *Mount Fuji and Mount Sinai*, 1984.

————, *Waterbuffalo Theology*, 1974.

Kozaki, Hiromichi, *The Essence of Christianity* (Kirisutokyō no Honshitsu), 1911.

————, *Liberal Theology* (Jiyū Shingaku), 1892.

————, *A New Essay on Politics and Religion* (Seikyō Shinron), 1886.

————, *The Present and Future of Christianity in Japan* (Nihon Genkon no Kirisutokyō narabini Shōrai no Kirisu tokyō), 1891.

Kumano, Yoshitaka, *The Basic Questions of Christology* (Kirisutoron no Konponmondai), 1934.

————, *Church and Creed* (Kyōkai to Shinjō), 1942.

————, *Contemporary Theology* (Gendai no Shingaku), 1934.

————, *Dogmatics* (Kyōgigaku), 3 vols., 1954, 1959, 1965.

————, *Eschatology and the Philosophy of History* (Shūmatsuron to Rekishi-tetsugaku), 1933.

————, *The Essence of Christianity* (Kirisutokyō no Honshitsu), 1949.

————, *Faith and Reality* (Shinkō to Genjitsu), 1941.

————, *The Faith of the Apostle Paul* (Shito Pauro no Shinkō), 1941.

————, *History of Japanese Christian Theological Thought* (Nihon Kirisutokyō Shingaku Shisōshi), 1968.

————, *Introduction to Christian Ethics* (Kirisutokyō Rinri Nyūmon), 1960.

————, *Introduction to Dialectical Theology* (Benshōhōteki Shingaku Gairon), 1932.

————, *Martin Luther* (Maruchin Rutā), 1947.

————, *The Outline of Christianity* (Kirisutokyō Gairon), 1947.

————, *The Problems of New Testament Theology* (Shinyaku Seishoshingaku no Shomondai), 1943.

————, *A Study of Johannine Epistles* (Yohane Shokan no Kenkyū), 1934.

————, *The Synoptic Gospels* (Kyōkan Fukuinsho), 1952.

————, *Troeltsch* (Toreruchi), 1944.

————, *The Uniqueness of Christianity* (Kirisutokyō no Tokuisei), 1941.

Kumazawa, Yoshinobu, *Bultmann* (Burutoman), 1962.

Kurosaki, Kōkichi, *New Testament Commentaries* (Chūkai Shinyakuseisho), 1929-50.

————, *New Testament Concordance* (Shinyakuseisho Goku Sakuin).

————, *Old Testament Short Commentaries* (Kyūyakuseisho Ryakkai), 3 vols., 1950.

151

Kuwada, Hidenobu, *Christian Theology in Outline* (Kirisutokyō Shingaku Gairon), 1941.
————, *Dialectical Theology* (Benshōhōteki Shingaku), 1933.
————, *The Essence of Christianity* (Kirisutokyō no Honshitsu), 1932.
————, *Understanding of Theology* (Shingaku no Rikai), 1939.
Marata, Tsutomu, *History of the Reformation* (Shūkyo Kaikakushi), 1909.
Maruyama, Masao, *Thought of Japan* (Nihon no Shisō), 1960.
Matsuki, Jisaburō, *The Epistle to the Romans* (Rōmabito eno Tegami), 1966.
————, *Man and Christ* (Ningen to Kirisuto), 1961.
————, *New Testament Theology* (Shinyaku Shingaku), 1972.
————, *The Relation between Jesus and the New Testament* (Iesu to Shinyakuseisho tono Kankei), 1980.
Matsunaga, Shin-ichi, *The Body and Ethics* (Karada to Rinri), 1976.
Miyamoto, Takenosuke, *The Basic Problems of Christian Ethics* (Kirisutokyō Rinrigaku no Konponmondai), 1939.
————, *The Basic Problems of the Philosophy of Religion* (Shūkyō Tetsugaku no Konponmondai), 1968.
————, *Hatano Seiichi*, 1965.
————, *The Image of Man in Modern Christianity* (Gendai Kirisutokyō no Ningenzō), 1958.
————, *The Logic of Religious Life* (Shūkyōteki Sei no Ronri), 1949.
————, *Philosophy as Symbol* (Shōchō to shiteno Tetsugaku), 1948.
————, *The Philosophy of Religion* (Shūkyō Tetsugaku), 1942.
Morita, Yūzaburō, *Modernity of Christianity* (Kirisutokyō no Kindaisei), 1973.
Mutō, Kazuo, *Between Theology and Philosophy of Religion* (Shingaku to Shūkyōtetsugaku no Aida), 1961.
————, *A New Possibility of the Philosophy of Religion* (Shūkyōtetsugaku no Atarashii Kanōsei), 1974.
————, *Philosophy of Religion* (Shūkyōtetsugaku), 1955.
————, *Theological and Philosophical Essays* (Shingakuteki, Shūkyōtetsugakuteki Ronshū), 2 vols., 1980, 1986.
Nakajima, Shigeru, *Biblical Jesus and Modern Thinking* (Seisho no Iesu to Gendai no Shii), 1965.
————, *The Essence of Social Christianity: The Religion of Redemptive Love* (Shakaiteki Kirisutokyō no Honshitsu: Shokuzai Ai no Shūkyō), 1937.
————, *God and Community* (Kami to Kyōdōshakai), 1929.
————, *Social Christianity and the New Experience of God* (Shakaiteki Kirisutokyō to Atarashii Kami no Taiken), 1931.
Nakazawa, Kōki, *Studies on Deutero-Isaiah* (Daini Izaya no Kenkyū), 1963.
Namiki, Kōichi, *Ancient Israel and Its Surroundings* (Kodai Isuraeru to sono Shūhen), 1979.

Nishimura, Toshiaki, *Prophecy and Wisdom in the Old Testament* (Kyūyaku-Seisho no Yogen to Chie), 1981.

Noro, Yoshio, *Existential Theology* (Jitsuzonronteki Shingaku), 1964.

————, *Existential Theology and Ethics* (Jitsuzonronteki Shingaku to Rinri), 1970.

————, *John Wesley: His Life and Theology* (Wesley no Shōgai to Shingaku), 1975.

Odagaki, Masaya, *God in Contemporary Thought* (Gendai Shisō no nakano kami), 1988.

————, *Hermeneutical Theology* (Kaishakugakuteki Shingaku), 1975.

————, *Philosophical Theology* (Tetsugakuteki Shingaku), 1983.

————, *To an Unknown God* (Shirarezaru Kami ni), 1980.

Odagiri, Nobuo, ed., *Study of Christology* (Kirisutoron no Kenkyū), 1968.

Ogawa, Keiji, *Subject and Transcendence* (Shutai to Chōetsu), 1975.

Ohki, Hideo, *Barth* (Baruto), 1984.

————, *Brunner* (Barunna), 1962.

————, *The Ethical Thought of Puritanism* (Pyuritanizumu no Rinrishisō), 1966.

Otsuka, Setsuji, *Christian Anthropology* (Kirisutokyō Ningengaku), 1948.

————, *Outline of Christianity* (Kirisutokyō Yōgi), 1971.

————, *Prolegomena to Christian Ethics* (Kirisutokyō Rinrigaku Josetsu), 1935.

Ouchi, Saburo, and Arimichi Ebisawa, *History of Christianity in Japan* (Nihon Kirisutokyōshi), 1970.

Saba, Wataru, ed., *Masahisa Uemura and His Age* (Masahisa Uemura to sono Jidai), vols. 7.

Sakon, Kiyoshi, *Study of the Psalms* (Shihen Kenkyū), 1972.

Satake, Akira, *The Apostle Paul* (Shito Pauro), 1981.

————, *The Epistle to the Galatians* (Garateabito eno Tegami), 1974.

————, *The Epistle to the Philippians* (Piripibito eno Tegami), 1969.

Satō, Shigehiko, *Luther's Basic Thoughts on Romans* (Rōmasho ni arawareshi Ruttā no Konponshisō), 1933.

————, *A Study of the Religion of Experience* (Taiken Shūkyō no Kenkyū), 1924.

————, *Young Luther* (Wakaki Rūteru), 1920.

Satō, Toshio, *The Loss and Restoration of Religion* (Shūkyo no Sōshitsu to Kaifuku), 1978.

————, *Modern Theology* (Kindai no Shingaku), 1964.

Sekine, Masao, *Commentary on Jeremiah* (Eremiasho), 1964.

————, *Commentary on Job* (Yobuki), 1970.

————, *Commentary on the Psalms* (Shihen), 1971.

————, *The History of the Religion and Culture of Israel* (Isuraeru-Shūkyō Bunkashi), 1952.

————, *History of Old Testament Literature* (Kyūyakuseisho Bungakushi), 2 vols., 1978, 1980.

————, *The Old Testament: Its History, Literature and Thought* (Kyūyakuseisho, sono Rekishi, Bungaku, Shisō), 1955.

————, *The Thinkers of Ancient Israel* (Kodai Isuraeru no Shisōka), 1982.

————, *The Thought and Language of Israel* (Isuraeru no Shisō to Gengo), 1962.

Tagawa, Kenzo, *Commentary on Mark* (Maruko Fukuinsho Chūkaisho), vol. 1, 1972.

————, *A Man Called Jesus* (Iesu to yuu Otoko), 1980.

————, *A Phase of the History of Primitive Christianity* (Genshi Kirisutokyōshi no Ichidanmen), 1968.

Takagi, Mizutarō, *Great Dictionary of Christianity* (Kirisutokyō Daijiten), 1911.

Takakura, Tokutarō, *Evangelical Christianity* (Fukuinteki Kirisutokyō), 1927.

————, *Grace and Calling* (Onchō to Shōmei), 1925.

————, *Grace and Faithfulness* (Onchō to Shinjitsu), 1921.

————, *The Kingdom of Grace* (Onchō no Ōkoku), 1921.

Takeda, Kiyoko Chō, ed., *The Method and Object of History of Thought: Japan and Europe,* 1961.

Takenaka, Masao, ed., *Dialogue of Religion in the Modern Age* (Gendai ni okeru Shukyō no Taiwa), 1979.

Takizawa, Katsumi, *Buddhism and Christianity* (Bukkyō to Kirisutokyō), 1964.

————, *God in Contemporary Thought* (Gendai Shiso no naka no Kami), 1988.

————, *Philosophical Theology* (Tetsugakuteki Shingaku), 1983.

————, *A Study of Karl Barth* (Kāru Baruto Kenkyū), 1941.

Tominaga, Tokumaro, *A New Interpretation of Christianity* (Kirisutokyō Shinkai), 1909.

Tomura, Masahiro, *Japanese Fascism and the Problem of the Yasukuni Shrine* (Nihon no Fashizumu to Yasukuni Mondai), 1974.

Tsukamoto, Toraji, *Colloquial Translation of the New Testament with Explanation* (Fuentsuki Kōgoyaku Shinyakuseisho), 1944.

————, *A Table of the Differences in the Gospels* (Fukuinsho Idō Ichiran), 1951.

Uchimura, Kanzō, *How I Became a Christian,* 1895.

————, *Gesammelte Schriften* (Uchimura Kanzō Zenshū).

Uemura, Masahisa, *A Guide-Post to the Gospel* (Fukuin no Michishirube), 1885.

————, *The Outline of Truth* (Shinri Ippan), 1884.

Uoki, Tadakazu, *Christian Spiritual History: The Spirit of Calvin's Theology* (Kirisutokyō Seishinshi: Karuban Shingaku no Seishin), 1948.

————, *History of Modern German Protestant Theological Thought* (Kindai Doitsu Purotesutantokyō Shingaku Shisōshi), 1934.

————, *The Spiritual Tradition of Japanese Christianity* (Nihon Kirisutokyō no Seishinteki Dentō), 1941.

Watanabe, Zenda, *Before the Exodus* (Shutsu Ejiput Izen), 1972.

———, *The Canonicity of the Bible* (Seisho Seitenron), 1949.

———, *Interpretation of the Bible* (Seisho Kaishakuron), 1954.

———, *Introduction to Moses' Five Books* (Mōse Gosho Choron), 1949.

———, *The Theology of the Old Testament* (Kyūyakusho no Shingaku), 3 vols., 1921-24.

———, *Theology of the Bible* (Seisho Shingakuron), 1963.

Yagi, Seiichi, *Biblical Jesus and Modern Thinking* (Seisho no Iesu to Gendai no Shii), 1965.

———, *Contact Points between Buddhism and Christianity* (Bukkyō to Kirisu-tokyō no Setten), 1975.

———, *The Falsehood of Ego and Religion* (Jiga no Kyokō to Shūkyō), 1980.

———, *The Formation of New Testament Thought* (Shinyaku Shisō no Seiritsu), 1963.

———, *Jesus and Christ* (Iesu to Kirisuto), 1969.

———, *Jesus and Nihilism* (Iesu to Nihirizumu), 1979.

———, *Paul/Shinran, Jesus/Zen* (Pauro/Shinran, Iesu/Zen), 1983.

———, *The Philosophy of Front-Structure* (Furonto-kōzō no Tetsugaku), 1988.

———, *Where Can We Find God?* (Kami wa dokode miidasareruka?), 1977.

Yamamoto, Kanō, *Politics and Religion: How Did Barth Fight?* (Seiji to Shūkyō: Kāru Baruto wa dō tatakattaka?), 1947.

———, *The Theology of Heilsgeschichte* (Kyūsaishi no Shingaku), 1972.

Yamaya, Seigo, *Explanatory Bibliography of the New Testament* (Shinyaku Seisho Kaidai), 1943.

———, *The New Testament: New Translation and Exegesis* (Shinyaku Seisho, Shinyaku to Shakugi), 5 vols., 1930-48.

———, *New Testament Theology* (Shinyaku Seisho Shingaku), 1966.

———, *The Origin of Christianity* (Kirisutokyō no Kigen), 2 vols., 1957-59.

———, *The Theology of Paul* (Pauro no Shingaku), 1936.

Yoshimitsu, Yoshihiko, *The Basic Problems of Cultural Ethics* (Bunka Rinri no Konponmondai), 1936.

———, *Catholicism, Thomas, Newman* (Katorishizumu, Tomasu, Nyūman), 1934.

———, *The God of the Philosopher* (Tetsugakusha no Kami), 1947.

———, *The Idea of Culture and Religion* (Bunka to Shūkyō no Rinen), 1947.

———, *Mysticism and the Modern Age* (Shinpishugi to Gendai), 1952.

———, *Poetry and Love and Existence* (Shi to Ai to Jitsuzon), 1940.

———, *A Study of History of Modern Philosophy* (Kinsei Tetsugakushi Kenkyū), 1949.

———, *A Study of Medieval Geistesgeschichte* (Chūsei Seishinshi Kenkyū), 1948.

Index of Names

Abe, Masao, 96
Adler, F., 67
Akagi, Yoshimitsu, 72
Akaiwa, Sakae, 55, 89-91, 106
Akizuki, Ryomin, 96, 100
Aquinas, 79
Arai, Sasagu, 97, 105, 106-8
Ariga, Tetsutaro, 62, 64-65, 71
Asano, Junichi, 60-61
Ashida, Keiji, 54, 68
Augustine, 45

Baillie, John, 68
Ballagh, James H., 16, 49
Barth, Karl, 3, 6, 50, 53, 54, 55, 56, 58, 59, 65, 67, 70, 73, 74, 80-82, 84, 85, 87, 89, 90, 94, 96, 102, 113, 115, 117-18, 119, 124, 125, 126n2, 130-31, 132, 139, 144
Beecher, Henry W., 15
Bennett, John C., 69
Berdjajew, J., 103
Berdyaev, Nicholas, 70
Biedermann, Alois E., 29

Böhme, J., 103
Bonhoeffer, Dietrich, 3, 85
Bousset, W., 44
Braun, Herbert, 120
Brown, Samuel R., 17, 49
Brown, W., 67
Brunner, Emil, 36, 53, 54, 56, 59, 67, 69, 70, 80-82, 85, 113
Buber, Martin, 102
Bultmann, Rudolf, 82, 85, 97, 100, 102
Bushnell, Horace, 15

Caldarola, Carlo, 36
Calvin, John, 49, 63, 64, 66, 76, 77
Choisy, E., 76
Chuang-tsze, 133
Clark, William S., 18
Clement of Alexandria, 62
Cobb, John, Jr., 135
Confucius, 15
Conzelmann, Hans, 105
Cox, H., 85

Deissmann, Adolf, 44

LaVergne, TN USA
19 August 2009
155287LV00004B/265/A